12·12·12

To: Dr. Bhao

In recognition of your _____,
organization and enthusiasm
throughout the Leadership 510
course. Thank you for
being a shining example
of leadership.

Respectfully,

Team Tangram
Mingming
Masha
Nael
&
John

SAM LOYD'S
book of tangrams

SAM LOYD'S
book of tangrams

Sam Loyd

With an Introduction and Solutions by
Peter Van Note

DOVER PUBLICATIONS, INC.
Mineola, New York

Bibliographical Note

This Dover edition, first published in 1968 and republished in 2007, is an unabridged republication of the work originally published by Loyd & Company in 1903. The 1968 Dover edition was published under the title *The Eighth Book of Tan* and added a new introduction and solutions prepared by Peter Van Note.

Library of Congress Cataloging-in-Publication Data

Loyd, Sam, 1841–1911.
   [8th book of tan]
   Sam Loyd's book of tangrams / Sam Loyd ; with an introduction and solutions by Peter Van Note.
      p. cm.
   Originally published: The 8th book of tan. 1968. With new introd.
   ISBN 0-486-45424-X
    1. Tangrams. I. Van Note, Peter. II. Title. III. Title: Book of tangrams.

GV1507.T3L6 2007
793.73—dc22

                                    2006103550

Manufactured in the United States of America
Dover Publications, Inc., 31 East 2nd Street, Mineola, N.Y. 11501

INTRODUCTION TO THE DOVER EDITION

When Sam Loyd was a small child, during the 1840's, a puzzle called the Chinese puzzle (which the French called the Chinese head-breaker, and we know today as the tangram) was the popular craze throughout Asia, Europe and the United States. The Chinese puzzle involved fitting a square, a parallelogram and five triangles together to form various patterns—of which hundreds were in circulation. "Young people are fond of puzzles, and have often puzzled for hours over bits of wood called Chinese puzzles, to very little purpose," complained an English children's magazine in 1844.

Nor were children alone in their fascination for the puzzle; among their elders, Napoleon Bonaparte, John Quincy Adams, Gustave Doré, Lewis Carroll and Edgar Allan Poe are all reputed to have "puzzled for hours" over their sets of tangrams. A French cartoonist depicted a family playing tangrams by dawn's early light, while affairs of the household went rapidly to pot.

The tangram sets most prized by nineteenth-century puzzle buffs were those imported from China; they were of ivory, and beautifully carved. Less elaborate and less costly were sets of wooden pieces, and many people simply cut their own sets of tangrams from squares of sturdy cardboard. Edgar Allan Poe owned one of the Chinese ivory sets; its seven pieces fitted together to form a square of 2 *ts'un* (about 2½ inches) to a side, and about one-eighth of an inch in thickness. Each piece, with its delicate openwork carving, was a picture in itself, with scenes of lucky cranes and smaller birds cavorting amid thickets of bamboo. Part of the puzzle was to figure out how to get the pieces back in their carved ivory box; the *outside* dimensions of the box, too, were about 2½ inches to a side, by about half an inch in thickness. Perhaps the reader can figure out how Poe put his set away for the night.

One eminent American tangram player of the nineteenth century was John Singer of Philadelphia, grandfather of painter John Singer Sargent. Singer collected two books of tangram patterns, which later passed on to his sister, Elizabeth Singer Loyd. She in turn passed them on to one of her sons, Sam Loyd.

Loyd recalled that his mother was "a devotee of the pastime, who took great delight in solving the puzzles and creating original designs." Of Loyd himself, a friend once wrote: "The fates had given him in large measure the endowment of genius. He could see at a glance what other people could see, or at least could be made to see, very slowly. . . . He could see an idea from many sides at once; first always from the point of view of a puzzle, then from the humorous standpoint, finally from the artistic aspect." Tangrams must have had a great appeal for Sam Loyd.

Yet it was not until 1903, when Loyd was sixty-one, that he finally got around to publishing his own book of tangram patterns. By then, of course, he had already triggered several puzzle crazes of his own invention—the Pony Puzzle, the 14-15 Puzzle, Pigs in Clover, the Trick Donkeys, among others. Even when allowing for a busy life, which included at various times careers in the music business, the plumbing business and the publishing business, the reason why Loyd waited from childhood to advanced years to write and publish his tangram book remains a minor mystery.

A possible explanation lies in his friendship with the English puzzle expert, Henry Ernest Dudeney. Loyd spent many of his hours corresponding with people who shared his interests, particularly where chess and puzzles were concerned, and Dudeney was among his correspondents. Some time around the turn of the century, Dudeney purchased a small book of tangram patterns at a sale of the estate of Lewis Carroll. (It was Carroll's book, by the way, that mentioned Napoleon as a tangram player.) In their

Part of the game of tangrams in the nineteenth century was to see who could solve a given "Chinese head-breaker" first. Papa is the winner in this French cartoon, but it took him all night to do it. (The same pattern is on page 20 of this book.)

letters, back and forth across the sea, Loyd and Dudeney undoubtedly talked of Dudeney's new acquisition, of tangrams in general, and probably even exchanged patterns, since at least one of the patterns in Loyd's book is known to have been of Dudeney's devising. Dudeney, it should be added, made free use of Loyd's patterns in his own books and articles. It may be that they had some exchange agreement between them.

Loyd called his book *The 8th Book of Tan, Part I*, promising his readers that Part II would be forthcoming. (So far as I know, this promise was never fulfilled, though I'm sure Loyd had good intentions.) He chose the title, he explained, because some four thousand years ago a Chinaman (or Chinese god) named Tan had compiled seven books of tangram patterns, of which—he said—only two were still extant. The two surviving books he had in mind, one suspects, were those handed down from Uncle John Singer. "The seven books of Tan," said Loyd, "were supposed to illustrate the creation of the world and the origin of species upon a plan which out-Darwins Darwin, the progress of the human race being traced through seven stages of development up to a mysterious state which is too lunatic for serious consideration."

With that statement, scholars like British philologist Sir James Murray should have been warned. In his own special way, Loyd blended half-truths and popular suppositions about things Oriental with a few figments of his own imagination; to this he added a few well-dropped names, and with a twinkle in his eye served the old puzzle up in a delightful mock-serious stew. Had Sir James looked more closely, he might have realized that Loyd's whole essay was "too lunatic for serious consideration." Instead, Sir James embarked on a search for the historical Tan. "One of my sons," he wrote some years later, "is a professor in the Anglo-Chinese college at Tientsin. Through him, his colleagues, and his students, I was able to make inquiries as to the alleged Tan among Chinese scholars. Our Chinese professor here [at Oxford] also took an interest in the matter and obtained information from the secretary of the Chinese Legation in London, who is a very eminent representative of the Chinese literati. The result has been to show that the man Tan, the god Tan, and the 'Book of Tan' are entirely unknown to Chinese literature, history, or tradition."

This is not to say that the puzzle, itself, was not known to the Chinese. Indeed, it was—and is—well known to them as the puzzle of "seven clever pieces." In addition to puzzle sets in wood or ivory, Chinese friends tell me of having seen or owned sets of dishes, lacquer boxes, and even small tables in the shapes of the seven pieces in China's pre-Communist days. While evidence of the puzzle's origin is scanty, it appears that it was enjoying a vogue in China around the turn of the nineteenth century, shortly before it first became popular in Europe and America. I own an 1854 reprint of a book of Chinese patterns, written originally during the reign of the Emperor Chia Ching (1796-1820); in his introduction, the author, who called himself "Guest under the Mulberry," tells how he came to compile the book:

The game of Seven Clever Pieces [tangrams] is also known as Making Patterns. It is so-called because the game involves shifting seven pieces about and fitting them together to make pictures.

Last year, Tsui Shu Tang of Yun Chien copied the patterns for more than 160 tangrams he had seen, and had them published for sale. I have not yet seen them.

But last summer, Yi Yuan brought a set of patterns from his home town to Soochow. To his collection, he added those devised by his brother, Chun Sang—making a total of more than 200 tangram patterns—all of which he showed to me.

As we had nothing better to do, my comrades and I began exploring the game, and we found its possibilities to be without limit. Acting on my suggestion, we added more than 100 additional patterns, and compiled the entire collection in one manuscript.

Rather than keep them to ourselves, we wish to share these patterns with all who are interested in tangrams. For this reason, we have submitted our manuscript for publication.

Like the antiquity of the puzzle, a question that may never be resolved for certain is the origin of the puzzle's name, tangram. Loyd, of course, did not invent the word; its first recorded use is in the 1864 edition of Webster's *Dictionary*. It has been suggested that the word might have been coined by some American or British toymaker, but, so far as I know, this has not been proved. Sir James Murray thought the word might have been formed by prefixing the Chinese word *t'an*, to extend, or *t'ang*, Cantonese dialect for Chinese, to the suffix, –gram. Obviously, there is room for further speculation.

Webster's first use of the word tangram suggests that it is probably of American coinage. Perhaps it would be worthwhile to ask, what were Americans doing in China around the turn of the nineteenth century? The first Yankee ships in Chinese waters, following the American Revolution, were freebooters; together with the Portuguese, Dutch, English, French and Spanish, they partook of the lucrative Far Eastern trade in tea, silk, rhubarb, and other exotic goods. But their most profitable business was the business of smuggling opium into China.

Not surprisingly, the records of these activities are few, but enough is known to suggest how American and European sailors might have acquired the game (and the name) of tangrams. With typical Oriental suspicion of "foreign devils," the Emperor in 1745 had ordered all Chinese ports closed to foreign commerce, save only the port of Canton. At Canton, trading for most goods was permitted without restriction, but an import duty was placed upon opium—about five dollars for the amount a man could carry on his back. This duty, of course, only served to encourage smuggling. Located some forty miles up the Pearl River from the open sea, Canton was not directly accessible to foreign shipping; above Whampoa, the river became too shallow for the deep-draft ocean-going boats. At Whampoa, the merchant ships had to transfer their cargo to shallow-bottomed Chinese river craft, which carried the goods the remaining nine miles to the *hongs*, warehouses maintained by the Americans and Europeans along Canton's river's edge.

With the transferal of legitimate wares by day, and opium by night, American and European sailors came to know the Chinese river boats well; whole families lived on these boats, were born on them and died on them. In Chinese, these dwellers-on-the-river were called *tanka*. In addition to mercantile services, tanka women took in laundry for the foreign sailors, whereas their daughters entertained them at night. (For whatever it's worth, a Chinese word for prostitute is *tan*.) It cannot be proved for certain, but it seems a fair guess that the tanka girls might have taught the sailors the puzzle of seven pieces, and that the "tanka game" might have become "tangram."

In compiling his book of tangrams, Loyd made no claim to having originated any of them, though it is clear that some of the best—for instance, the Indian and his squaw on page 31—are his. Surprisingly, some of the most modern-looking of Loyd's patterns are actually Chinese; some of buildings on page 10 are called "foreign buildings" in old Chinese collections, and probably represent some of the *hongs* at Canton and Macao. The mysterious Monad sign, several times cited by Loyd, is called a "peach" in my Chinese book. Loyd was fond of puzzles based on paradoxes and unexpected solutions; the reader can expect to find these aplenty in this book. His pair of top-spinners on page 27 is an example; Loyd asks us whether the "top" belongs to the first or second player, or whether it is an independent piece. We quickly discover that the first player is comprised of six pieces, so the top must belong to him; and the second player must be made up of seven pieces. But no matter how we try, the seven pieces do not quite conform to the pattern. Loyd's method (or the method I think he used) is not quite fair, but I hope the reader can figure it for himself without turning to the solution on page 51.

Regarding the solutions, Loyd compiled well over six hundred patterns in his book, of which we have broken all but a small handful. Of these, a few would seem not to be true tangrams; that is, they seem to require more or fewer pieces than the full seven-piece tangram set, or some such maneuver as substituting a second middle-sized triangle for the parallelogram. However, I am not prepared to label any of these patterns as "impossible"; it is said that a tangram once declared by an expert as impossible was promptly solved in thirty-nine seconds by a ten-year-old Girl Scout. The reader may enjoy tackling these as yet unsolved problems for himself.

Several friends shared in the fun of making this new edition of Loyd's book possible. Dr. Frank Yee translated a number of old Chinese manuscripts quickly, and I believe accurately. Martin Gardner gave continual encouragement, and suggested some fruitful leads for research. Miss Edythe Bull, one of the sharpest tangram players I know, was generous in lending books from her collection and in solving some of Loyd's more interesting patterns. To these people, many thanks. But my deepest thanks to Tan—whoever he was—for starting a good thing.

PETER VAN NOTE

New York, New York
January, 1968

FURTHER READING ON TANGRAMS

Considering the long history and popularity of the puzzle, the literature of tangrams is remarkably small, and much of it appallingly trivial. The following books, however, all currently available, are particularly recommended.

Amusements in Mathematics, Henry E. Dudeney (Dover). A classic puzzle potpourri. In an amusing prologue to an ingenious tangram "paradox," he includes about two dozen delightful patterns, most of them of his own devising. Perhaps to perpetuate the joke, Dudeney repeats Loyd's account of the "Seven Books of Tan."

The 2nd Scientific American Book of Mathematical Puzzles & Diversions, Martin Gardner (Simon & Schuster), based upon the author's entertaining "Mathematical Games" columns. Mathematical sidelights of tangrams are discussed in one chapter; illustrated with 16 patterns.

Tangrams, 330 Puzzles, Ronald C. Read (Dover). The limitless possibilities of the puzzle are an obvious fascination to Read, and he explores them with great relish. For the most part, his patterns are from Loyd, Chinese manuscripts, or of his own excellent invention. A chapter on the Chinese 15-piece tangram is an unusual and welcome feature. Solutions included.

Tangrams, Picture-Making Puzzle Game, Peter Van Note (Tuttle). The artistic side of the puzzle is shown through more than 100 patterns combined into 20 lively tangram tableaux. About half the patterns are from Dudeney's puzzle columns of the old *Strand* magazine, making this possibly the largest collection of Dudeney's tangrams available. Solutions and a seven-piece set included.

The cover design of the original edition.

CHINESE TANGRAMS
BY SAM LOYD

ACCORDING to encyclopædia lore, the game of Tangrams is of very ancient origin, and has been played in China for upward of 4,000 years, somewhat in the nature of a national pastime. It consists of seven flat pieces of wood, cut upon the geometrical angles of 45 and 90 degrees, with straight edges which fit together so as to produce a variety of changes which baffles the science of mathematics to compute.

Webster's dictionary merely mentions Tangrams as being used in primary schools for elementary kindergarten instruction. According to one authority, "the simple shapes are eminently suitable for illustrating a limited number of plane geometrical figures."

The aim of this work is to show the unlimited range of those possibilities, and to explain, in the language of truthful James:

" Which I wish to remark—
And my language is plain—
That for ways that are dark
And for tricks that are vain,
The heathen Chinee is peculiar :
Which the same I would rise to explain.''

There are so many popular editions printed in puzzle-book form that it is safe to say that it is known throughout the entire world as a very simple little pastime, suitable for the juveniles. Through that unfortunate misconception of the scope of the science, as it should be termed, it has failed to be properly appreciated.

The finest figures have been thrown out as impossible of construction, and the important and fascinating feature of originating new designs entirely omitted.

In this feeble attempt to do justice to the grandeur of the original conception, it must be understood that each and every one of the illustrations requires a complete set of Tangrams. It constitutes, therefore, a unique collection of puzzles, wherein the object is to guess the names of the subjects; to discover their construction and penetrate the mysteries which surround them, as well as to originate new and artistic designs with the same limited number of pieces.

At first we are amazed at the unfitness of the shapes of the pieces with which we are expected to accomplish so much. The number seven is an obstinate prime which cannot be divided into symmetrical halves; and the geometrical forms, all alike, with harsh angles, preclude the possibility of variety, curves, or graceful lines.

Many puzzlists have invented cut-up pictures, where twenty or more pieces are to be put together to make some form, which is not so unique as many of these. No genius has ever been able to make a good puzzle where pieces refit together, so as to make a second object, and yet here are only seven angular pieces, which, without any omissions, duplications or lapping of edges, give free rein to the imagination, to produce ten thousand different designs.

According to the late Professor Challenor, whose posthumous papers have come into the possession of the writer, seven books of Tangrams, containing one thousand designs each, are known to have been compiled in China over 4,000 years ago. These books are so rare that Professor Challenor says that during a forty years' residence in China he only succeeded in seeing perfect editions of the first and seventh volumes, with stray fragments of the second. In this connection it may be mentioned that portions of one of the books, printed in gold-leaf upon parchment, were found in Pekin by an English soldier and sold for £300 to a collector of Chinese antiquities, who kindly furnished some of the choicest designs presented in this work. According to Professor Challenor, the many specimens of Tangrams which have been published from time to time in small volumes, in the form of well-known collections, are extracts from what might be termed Chinese catechisms, designed to elucidate the different features of the original works. Of these small books there are about twenty varieties, limited, however, to a selection of the poorest and less important subjects, after the following symmetrical style, as the publishers merely present them in the nature of juvenile puzzles.

The seven Books of Tan were supposed to illustrate the creation of the world and the origin of species upon a plan which out-Darwins Darwin, the progress of the human race being traced through seven stages of development up to a mysterious spiritual state which is too lunatic for serious consideration.

Here are some specimens from the first book, which may possibly relate to what Huxley would term the era of protoplasm, as they do not suggest anything else that can be thought of.

Professor Challenor mentions that the first figure in each of the original works is evidently designed to represent the Chinese Monad or symbol of Deity, but gives a mistaken interpretation of the next figures as pertaining to a chaotic era. The second form is evidently designed to give the white part of the symbol surrounded by black. (See the sign of the Monad as given on the illustrated title-page.) The Rev. Dr. Holt, who discovered that the Northern Pacific Railroad had unwittingly adopted the Monad as their seal, describes the parts as the Yen and Yin, representing the male and female principles of Chinese cosmogony. I am indebted to Chief Engineer McHenry, of the N. P. Railroad, for much valuable information on the subject.

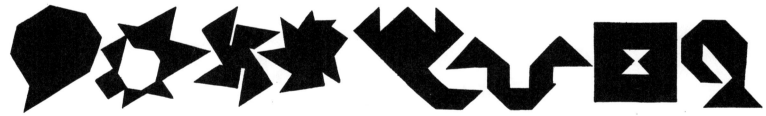

In speaking of Chinese philosophy, Dr. Scott says: "They claim that the illimitable produced the extreme; the great extreme the two principles; the two principles produced the four dimensions, and from the four dimensions were developed what the Chinese call the eight diagrams of Feu-hi, over 3,000 years ago." All of which may be made to appear more tangible later on.

Alongside of the Monad stands the Swastika symbol, which Professor Thomas Wilson, of the Smithsonian Institute, proves, in his great work of 500 illustrations, to be the oldest human symbol known to science. It means in Sanskrit, "good fortune." But Professor Whitney, the profound archæologist, explains its definition in Chinese to mean "many long years." The other figures which follow may represent chaos, as suggested by Professor Challenor, or pertain to ancient symbols of unknown significance; but it is a fact that Dr. Schliemann, in his excavations of the seven ancient cities, found many well-defined figures, like the following, which appear in the popular collections of Tangrams:

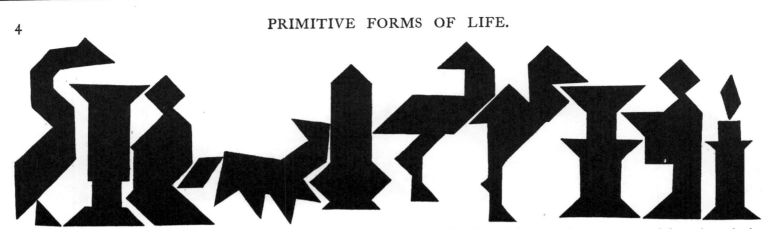

There is a popular little evolution word-game, to convert one word into another through a chain of proper words by merely changing one letter at a time; as, for example, to turn ape into man by seven changes—ape, aye, dye, die, din, Dan, man. This puzzle-game gives an excellent idea of the Chinese connecting links in the development of species. There being seven pieces in each design makes it possible by the slightest change to bring about a resemblance to some other object. So we are thus led by a connecting chain through all the species of birds, animals, and fishes, and, as a matter of fact, through the whole category of everything else. In many instances we are confronted by a clever puzzle in the nature of a challenge to discover the best connecting link between two forms.

The opening pages of the first book of Tan illustrate the primitive forms of life, by the following weird specimens of germs, wiggles, and squirmers, which might readily be taken for Professor Koch's latest discoveries of microbes and bacilli, or a microscopical exhibit of the inhabitants of a drop of water.

The successive stages of development would seem to indicate that our great-grandfather, after sporting in the guise of tadpoles, skimmers, eels, and lobsters, evolved through a school of fishes, just as tangible as that described by Lewis Carroll in "Alice in Wonderland," and made his début upon land in the form of a tortoise:

After sporting in the form of insects, birds, and animals, through progressive chains of evolutions which savor of pagan mythology, the connecting link of our ancestral baboon is strongly in evidence, as shown in the fraternal greeting of the monkey man:

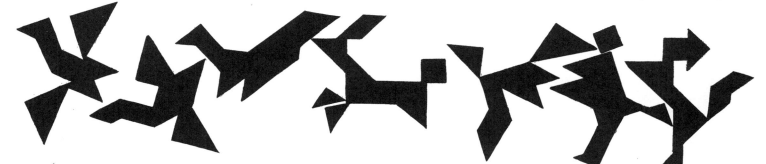

It is worthy of note that the Rev. Dr. Holt says, in his recently published interview, that Chinese research has "caused many philosophers to speculate as to whether the cosmogonies and theologies of the western nations did not originate in the Orient."

That everything emanates from God Tan, and is endowed with the "seven attributes," to say the least, is unique and logical, for each figure being constructed out of the same seven pieces makes the transition from one to another an easy one. The remarkable fact of each piece being susceptible of subdivision into a set of smaller tangrams, and that any figure may be built larger by the addition of extra sets, is held to represent the principle of growth in nature, as well as the problem of infinity, somewhat according to Dean Swift's famous interpretation:

" Great fleas have little fleas upon their backs to bite 'em,
  As little fleas have lesser fleas, and so ad infinitum.
  And the great fleas in turn have greater fleas to go on :
  While these again have greater still, and greater still, and so on."

We are then introduced to a number of crude and misshapen figures of men and women, which, through a gradual change of forms and fashions of costumes, develop into graceful posings and groups, which display considerable artistic ability and sense of humor.   Many of the designs, supposed to be illustrative of the advancement of the human race, are weird centaur-looking combinations with different animals, possibly representing connecting links of evolution, with which the ancients were more familiar than the present generation.   In three instances are to be found the combination of a goose or duck with what has been taken to be a flying squirrel, probably to show a certain connection between water, air, and earth.

Here are the first four representations of the human race, followed by others which show a gradual improvement in form.

That these primitive and imperfect representations of men and animals are purposely crude and distorted is self-evident from the fact of their being reproduced afterward with a perfection and regard for the details and characteristics of the subjects which challenges our admiration.

The theory of the connection links between the various forms of life clearly antedates Darwin, Haeckel, and Huxley by some thousands of year, just as in a similar way it can be proven that Archimedes, Pythagoras, and Euclid must have known of the second book of Tan, which deals largely in matters of trigonometry and geometry in a way that clearly anticipates the claims of those great mathematicians.

The famous 47th problem of Euclid, known as *Pons Asinorum,* and the familiar illustrations of hexagons, triangles, rhomboids, and polygons, are identical with the second book of Tan.

It is well known that one of Euclid's books, which is said to have been lost, was devoted to fallacies, tricks, and impossible problems, for the pupils to detect the errors.   The greater part of the second book of Tan is built upon similar surprises or illusions of a subtle nature.   Many of these problems are intentionally impossible of solution, or at least beyond the ability of the writer, while others are given on a deceptive scale of size which misleads the eye.   There is also a curious trick connected with many of the forms, necessitating the turning over of the rhomboid piece, which is very tantalizing.   It may be said incidentally that the antiquity or position of some of the designs can be approximately determined by these tricky features, which occur only in the first two books.

These puzzles, mathematical problems, and fallacies are treated more fully later on; but, as a few words of explanation at this point will be of assistance, we will take a look at the following display of shoes, wherein the turning over of the rhomboid piece has to be utilized. In the "tailor's gooses" we have a simple version of the paradoxical fallacies which will be introduced again in more difficult form. The first, as may be seen, is constructed with seven pieces, while the other one, supposed to be of the same form and size in every respect, is built with only six pieces and has a superfluous triangle. It being self-evident that the same form and dimensions cannot be constructed with a different number of pieces, we are asked to determine which is correct.

The Chinese are wonderfully prolix in the treatment of a subject, and will ring the changes upon every possible variation, as if it was an all-important point to show that a certain figure can be constructed in many different ways. The designs of the six shoes are taken from a Chinese book published in Canton in 1690, which shows three styles of heels, six kinds of toes, and six different tops, all of which being interchangeable upon a permutative basis should produce 108 different styles, more or less, and we are coolly asked to guess the possible number of changes!

In many instances the designs are marked with a number, which is supposed to tell in how many different ways the same object can be constructed or varied.

Connecting Li Hung Chang's statement that he "knew all the figures of the seven books of Tan before he could talk," with his remarkable and hitherto unexplained reference to Tangrams as being "a progressive philosophy with seven interpretations," we get some idea of the scope of the work as described by Professor Challenor. He says that Confucius makes several allusions to Tangrams, which he likens to "a game where the babes learn the form of things; youths exercise their wits; men study mathematics; artists get designs; poets fire the imagination, and the wise ponder over the past, present, and future."

The philosopher Choofootze is said to have discoursed at length upon "the seven interpretations of Tangrams," although the same does not appear in any of the wise sayings ascribed to him; so we are compelled to accept the views of Confucius, which were so happily endorsed by Li Hung Chang in his description of the pastime.

Many of the forms may readily be named, yet we detect a certain progressive degree of difficulty, suggestive of a puzzle feature combined with a very instructive school of design. It may be of interest at the present stage of the game to challenge the reader to guess the following subjects, which will be referred to again as pertaining to an important feature of the work:

It can be proven that the seven volumes were written at different periods, and Professor Challenor, who was a life-long enthusiast upon the subject, attempts to give some idea of the date of their appearance, and quotes, in support of his argument, a well-known Chinese saying which speaks of "the fool who would write the eighth book of Tan." This does not harmonize altogether with his description of the seven volumes as one complete inseparable scheme wherein the first imperfect forms are to be reproduced afterward.

As a matter of fact, it would appear as if Tangrams might be studied to advantage from any number of different standpoints. Gustave Doré, whose power of imagery was almost akin to madness, first developed his love of art by designing figures with the seven magical pieces.

Lewis Carroll, who had the temerity and power of imagination to portray the vagaries of dreamland, was a votary of the pastime, and when he became the profound professor of mathematics at Oxford University was wont to employ the seven pieces to expound the problems of Euclid.

It may be mentioned that at a recent sale of Lewis Carroll's library there was purchased by Henry C. Dudeney, the noted puzzlist, a little work, entitled "The Fashionable Chinese Puzzle," containing 323 designs in tangrams. It was issued at a place called Sidmouth, England, and we get an approximate date of publication from the following interesting bit of information taken from the introduction: "This ingenious contrivance has for some time past been the favorite amusement of the ex-Emperor Napoleon, who, being now in a debilitated state, and living very retired, passes many hours a day in thus exercising his patience and ingenuity."

Just imagine the great fighter finding relaxation for his tired brain in illustrating the incidents of his eventful career. We wonder if it ever occurred to him to portray that disastrous retreat from Moscow after the following manner:

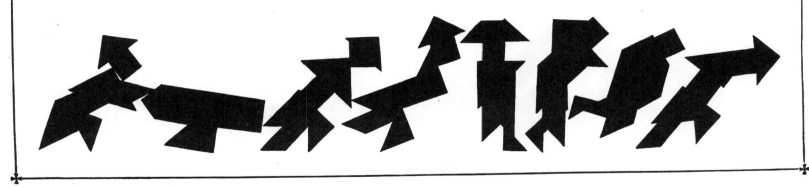

The dawn and advance of civilization is not confined to any one chapter or portion of a book, but extends throughout the entire work, portraying, in all its minutest details, the different phases of progress. Justice to this grand feature of a scheme, requiring over 7,000 illustrations to harmonize and connect the gradual changes, cannot be expected in this brief synopsis. Nothing but the importance of the subject induces the writer to dare the attempt, with the meagre resources at his command, so he depends largely upon the kind indulgence and vivid imaginations of his readers.

The following ten designs are taken from a collection of several hundred unique specimens of the more advanced implements, utensils, and vases, which are supposed to show a certain improvement on the crude articles given below:

The progress of architecture is given at great length, not confined to one page, but scattered throughout the work, beginning with the primitive homes, tents, and huts of the mound-builders up to the development of the chimney, as shown:

Assuming that enough has been said to show that the mere solving of puzzles is the least important feature of Tangrams, we will resume the historical thread from the point where primitive man made his appearance. Antiquarians and archæologists will have an opportunity to revel in what may be presented as the oldest known illustrations of utensils, weapons, and articles of pottery and stoneware of the prehistoric age. These designs appear in all puzzle-book editions, and are familiar as pertaining to geometrical figures which have been studied for many centuries simply in the nature of puzzles.

From the primitive cabin of our prehistoric ancestors we are led, by gradual and interesting stages, through an architectural course up to pretentious residences, towers, pagodas, forts, tem- ples, and palaces, characteristic of the style of the Celestials of more recent dates, specimens of which are here shown, without reference to the question of improvement:

In the matter of interior decorations for the house, as well as in furniture, utensils, chinaware, etc., the illustrations are profuse and marvellous in the minutiæ of details. Here, for example, is shown the plain old-fashioned open hearth which, through the evolutions of various styles, develops into a fireplace and mantel of artistic design:

As closely allied to the fortress and moated castle, here is an exhibition of masonry in the form of bridges and archways of varied design, which calls for clever handling of the pieces from a puzzle standpoint:

In the following additional specimens of bridge-building the first two were marked by a sign which has been interpreted as signifying "worthy of special notice." These signs, somewhat in the nature of exclamation marks, proved of great service in discovering hidden meanings or connections with other illustra- tions. In the first figure it may be intended to call attention to the fact of its being the same as a design shown elsewhere with- out the rhomboid piece removed. The second is the same as one of the primitive huts, with a mysterious addition on the top which is not easy of explanation:

There is a fine display of antique furniture, consisting of beds, chairs, sofas, lounges, tables, etc., some of such elaborate pattern as to be unintelligible to us Christians, so we will have to be satisfied with the following simple articles:

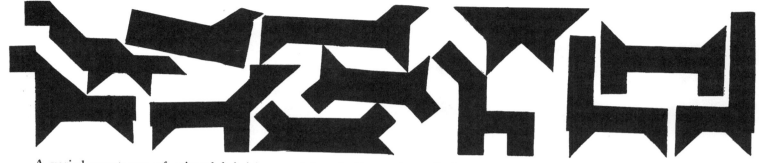

A varied assortment of oriental bric-à-brac and household goods, gathered at random from the later books of Tan, shows advancement from the primitive utensils already described. Each piece tells its own story without the necessity of further explanation, and will be readily recognized as belonging to the well-known forms in the popular editions of Tangrams:

The following glimpse of a Chinese clothes-line, presenting an array of the oldest designs, proves that the Celestial fashions have not undergone much change within the past few thousand years. Costumes of more elaborate design doubtless occur throughout the books, but as the writer makes no pretensions to be an expert sinologist it is safe to say that they have been presented as geometrical figures, wild animals, or some sort of household utensils:

The development of boat-building is well represented, and we are led by interesting steps through a regular course of naval architecture, from the primitive canoes, sailboats, barges, junks, and gondolas to stately merchant vessels and battle-ships. The following motley grouping of the more ancient illustrations is very suggestive of a night in Venice:

In the matter of regalia and decorations, which are of more importance to a Celestial than the rest of his clothes, there is a lavish display which embraces all of the emblems, signs, and banners of the thousand and one societies which infest the Flowery Kingdom. Here are a few of the most ancient insignias known, which, in the feature of ingenious puzzle construction, display considerable ingenuity and raise the question as to whether the signs of the different orders were designed from Tangrams or vice versa. Many of these figures may also be found among ancient Egyptian inscriptions:

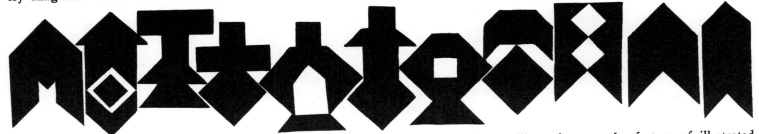

The original books of Tangrams were printed upon a fragile kind of rice-paper, and although reproduced at different periods it can be shown in every instance underwent such a considerable change and abbreviation as to mar the work and make it unreliable. The subject had come to be treated solely from the standpoint of a collection of puzzles, ignoring the construction of new illustrations, or the feature of illustrated narrative.

The pastime was evidently designed in its original form for educational purposes, and undoubtedly constituted a marvellous and instructive school of design, calculated to develop the imagination and a love of art. What drawing master does not aim to teach his pupils to produce desired effects by the fewest possible strokes of the pencil, just as we restrict the Tangram scholars to seven pieces with which to illustrate graceful posing or strong action, and that artistic *ligne* which the French rave about?

In but one solitary instance have I ever discovered an extraneous line added to the seven pieces, and, as the same occurs in the opening chapter as if in appeal to the reader's imagination, it is here used by way of explanation in the same way. A Tangramist must be able to picture those foils in his mind's eye, as well as the vexed expression of the lady whose escort is bowing so effusively; or the wearied look on the face of the stout old party with the flirtatious daughter.

Where is the artist who knows the power of black and white, the dark shadows and strong high lights, with the sharp silhouette effects like Gustave Doré, who said that he "loved Tangrams"? What painter, past or present, could produce such effects by so few touches of the magic brush as John Singer Sargent, the greatest portrait painter of the present day? Perhaps he was a student in the Tangram art school, for the two books of Tangrams which I possess came to me from his grandfather, John Singer, of Philadelphia, a brother of my own mother, who it may be said was a devoté of the pastime, who took great delight in solving the puzzles and creating original designs.

In corroboration of a statement ascribed to Professor Frederick Max Müller, that "the *science* of Tangrams gives evidence of a higher state of civilization than now exists in China," it may be said, without giving offence by mentioning names, that an eminent Chinese minister to this country held that "the early books of Tangrams had been superseded by improved versions, with the *crude* designs eliminated." All of which confirms Professor Challenor's opinion that the intent and original spirit of the work is practically unknown in China, and is no longer held in its former high esteem.

It being shown that the chief merit of the primitive forms depended upon their artistic crudeness, it may also be said that the many repetitions of the same designs pertain to different interpretations. The Monad sign, according to Professor Challenor, appears seven times in each book "in the nature of a period to close the chapter." In this respect it is safe to say he has overlooked one of the most unique and beautiful features of the work. The Monad sign whenever met should be taken in the sense of the D. C. al Sig. sign in music, viz., "return to sign at the beginning," and review from the new standpoint!

Anyway, that interpretation is here accepted, and the reader is always asked to turn back and review with the newly acquired information, and to kindly remember that the writer is attempting, with a few hundred illustrations, to give an inkling of the scope of a work which required 7,000.

The book should first be glanced over from the standpoint of a little child who loves funny pictures. He notices that some are better than others, and, be he young or old, he finds many of such poor construction as to tax the imagination at first. Then the work is reread with the knowledge that each subject is built with the same seven pieces, and that the contrary little pieces are to be converted into rounded forms and graceful curves. Then we detect a gradual and systematic improvement in the construction of the figures, and get some idea of the attempt to portray the development of species and the onward march of civilization as has been already explained.

The puzzle feature of discovering how to make any of the forms with the seven pieces must not be overlooked, for, while some of them are very easy, there are others so difficult that for hundreds of years they have been considered as impossible of solution.

It is believed that all of the designs presented in this work have been passed upon as correct, and will yield to patience and perseverance after one has become familiar with the shapes of the pieces.

At first some figures will be found which do not bear resemblance to any known object, and others will seem to be impossible of solution; and, when one essays his hand at creating new designs, it appears as if all of the good ideas were exhausted, and the obstinate little pieces, or the brain, cannot be induced to work properly.

Another reading of the book, and the solving of the puzzles will produce a wonderful change, so that one becomes astonished at the facility with which any subject which occurs to the mind can be faithfully represented.

It is at this stage of the game that it becomes necessary to check one's imagination, or in his enthusiasm he will fancy that the many things he sees must be just as plain to anyone else. As a matter of fact, to a beginner some of the finest designs are unintelligible, and some persons can never see anything but angles.

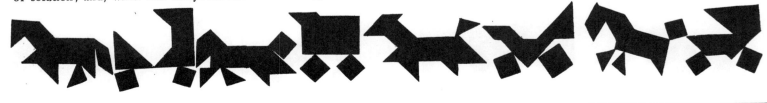

In learning to originate new designs, confine your efforts at first to simple figures which do not call for explanations as to whether they are animals or cooking utensils. Afterward you can essay designs which cater to the imagination, like the following illustration of Shakespeare's seven ages of man: from the puking babe, the unwilling schoolboy, the sighing lover, the quarrelsome soldier, the round-bellied justice, the lean slippered pantaloon and decrepit old age. It was deemed expedient to introduce the first figure of a policeman to suggest the nurse-maid, and the baby-carriage then serves as a preface to the "muling."

In portraiture there seems to have been a vast and interesting collection, but, unfortunately, the illustrations to which Professor Challenor's copious notes refer were lost with others of his most valuable papers. Only eleven of the faces are to be found, and as they are described as belonging to the barbaric age they are crude and not pretty to look at. The two which appear to be like busts upon pedestals are given as belonging to some clever representations of statuary.

The two Celestials with pig-tails are mentioned as showing the few illustrations of queues, which appear only in the last book, which is taken therefore to indicate that it must have been written during the Chow dynasty, 1,100 years before Christ.

In the following gallery we begin with a portrait of the old Scotch Piper, then the French Grenadier, and a Colonial General next to the Turk. Aunt Betsy with Uncle Rhube and Mary Smith, whom we all know, comes next, and then we have a head of John Knox. Tom Sharkey requires no introduction, and then we have the Professor, Buffalo Bill, and "the Easy Boss," all of whom it is safe to say could be recognized from the others.

It is a pity there should be such a meagre representation of this interesting and important feature. It has been shown that not only can people, birds, and animals be built up with the seven little pieces, but the same may be done so cleverly as to portray their characteristics and emotions. In the same way we can construct heads and faces, and, by a little artistic ability in the finishing touches, make the features and expressions readily recognizable.

The imagination may be strained pretty close to the snapping point to see some of these things, for they have been hastily and not too cleverly thrown together. There is room for improvement in every figure shown in this book, so it is safe to say there will be some wonderful pictures contributed after our young folks become experts, and I hope to see some great cartoonists and artists develop from our Tangram class.

The following scene represents some Chinese maidens playing foot-ball, which is closely akin to basket-ball, in that the aim is to place the ball upon the pedestal. They simply "punt," as "hacking" is not permitted. The only method of obstruction being to *butt* in a decorous manner, as shown in the sketch, where two girls are seen in a head-on collision, while the victor is supposed to be placing the ball upon the square pedestal:

Pictures in silhouette leave so much for the imagination that it is safe to say that no two persons ever get the same impressions from a Tangram sketch. They are given bold outlines in black and white of a subject which they are to complete according to their artistic ability or poetical inspiration.

Anyone who could look at groups of romping children without seeing in the mind's eye graceful curves and smiling faces is like that soul devoid of music, "fit for treason, stratagem, and spoils." Such as can only see angular shadows, or things actually shown, are so lacking in poetical imagination that they would read of "The little house where I was born" or of the Village Smithy "under a spreading chestnut-tree" with a shuddering sense of the lonesomeness of the situation. They see no groups of merry children or the panorama of busy life in all its little details, which a poet's theme inspires.

Here we have a group of marauding crows, with one or two excellent figures to support and interpret the rest. One of them was previously given without the supporting companions to see if it could be recognized when unaccompanied by explanatory description of any kind.

The imagination must be educated up to the point of seeing things which do not exist, so that our fancy fills in the lines and features necessary to complete the picture; then, after becoming expert in the handling of the Tangrams, we may essay the more difficult lines which challenge interpretation.

The latter books of Tan lead up to that phase by the ingenious and most skilfully devised grouping of subjects, so that you fail to notice how one or two good figures explain by asso-

ciation others which could not be guessed. This feature has been frequently introduced, but is now illustrated in a more pronounced form.

In similar vein is here presented a feline study in the shape of a pretty scene of a mother tabby and her family, to test the point as to how much poetry you have in your soul. Just observe the eyes and expressions of those mischievous kittens, and note the bristling whiskers!

Again, in the following companion picture, representing a rabbit-warren, much is left to the fancy of the student. The feature of one or two happy figures introducing the others, which are not so good, is once more utilized. Bunnies are not so pict-

uresque or graceful as kittens, so, as you will observe, I had to utilize their large eyes and soft fur in addition to the attitudes to give proper expression to rabbit emotions, which cannot be shown by the ears alone.

They speak a strictly monosyllabic language in China, and the same is written by a series of arbitrary word-signs, without attempt at alphabetical spelling; so, although it has been shown that the seven tangrams may be combined to form the rudimental words, there is practically no attempt at letter-press description

in the original books. It is plain, however, that there is a certain illustrative narrative, which, from the humorous postures, would suggest popular proverbs or fables rather than historical incidents. Be that as it may, however, according to Professor Challenor, such things pertained to unwritten legendry, and were irretrievably lost ages ago. He held that the same was of no great importance, and he aimed merely to revive the educational features of the work, which of necessity requires a certain modernizing of the whole scheme. As explanatory of the reference to illustrated fables we present the following up-to-date rendering of the famous nursery rhyme about

" The farmer who sowed the corn,
 That fed the cock that crowed in the morn,
 That woke the priest all shaven and shorn,
 That married the man all tattered and torn,
 That kissed the maiden all forlorn,
 That milked the cow with crumpled horn,
 That tossed the dog that worried the cat,
 That killed the rat that ate the malt
 That lay in the house that Vanderbilt."

We might also, by a slight effort of the imagination, amuse a group of children with a recital of the ever-popular story of Cinderella and the little glass slipper, with Tangram illustrations. Commencing, as shown, with the fireplace, Cinderella, the haughty sisters, the kind fairy, what might serve in a pinch for a pumpkin, the rat coachman, the little slipper, and finally the handsome prince doing a stately minuet with the heroine. The coach, horses, etc., are shown later on.

From a puzzlist's standpoint it would seem but fair to have the Tangrams drawn to a uniform scale of size, and modern publishers make the error of attempting to improve upon the Chinese plan. By so doing they eliminate the invaluable study of geometry which trains the eye to judge of the ratio of one piece to another, instead of solving puzzles by mechanical measurements of the lengths of the sides.

Artists who sketch from nature will best appreciate the feature of reducing in correct proportion where measurements are impossible.

Tangrams were never designed to be drawn upon a specified scale of size. Each design is to be made with a set of seven pieces which fit together to form a perfect square, but the pictures are not of the same size. By this means the Chinese conception of perspective is faithfully represented. They use flat colors or tints, and depend entirely upon the different sizes of the objects to represent distance. If such was not the case, in the story of the house that Jack built the cock that crowed in the morn would look bigger than the cow with crumpled horn, and the house would be smaller than the malt.

There are certain characteristics of form and action in animals and birds which may be studied to advantage by practice with Tangrams, and I have yet to discover any subject which cannot be fairly shown by the seven magic pieces. Some may be a little crude perhaps, but, if space permitted, it would be a simple matter to illustrate the entire list as given in the familiar rhyme of Noah's ark, where

> " Old Father Noah he built an ark,
> And covered it over with hickory bark.
>
> The animals walked in two by two,
> The elephant and the kangaroo.
>
> The animals walked in three by three,
> Two cats arm in arm with a humble bee.

The animals walked in four by four,
The big rhinoceros stuck in the door.

The animals walked in five by five,
The queen bee leading the rest of her hive.

The animals walked in six by six,
The squirrels and bunnies full of their tricks.

The animals walked in seven by seven,
Says the bug to the bear : ' Who are yer shovin' ? '

The animals walked in eight by eight,
Butted on by a goat, 'cause he thought they were late.

The animals walked in nine by nine,
The apes kicking up a big monkey shine.

The animals walked in ten by ten,
The fox with his eye on a big fat hen.''

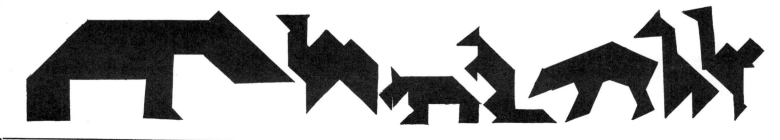

To reproduce another of the puzzling figures previously given, we will take a glance at the poultry-yard, where an idea of doubtful subjects may be gleaned by association with others.

Attention is incidentally called to the feature of a little gosling supposed to be feeding from a box, wherein the bird and the box are assumed to belong to the one design, so that both must be constructed with but seven pieces, although in some cases the box might constitute a separate subject.

This trick is a great feature in the Chinese books, and pertains to the mysterious and paradoxical construction of forms with a disappearing piece. In every instance, as in the scene of the girls playing foot-ball, the ball can be made out of seven pieces, or the pedestal can be made from seven, and yet in the final figure the two are combined so that both together are to be made from the same seven pieces.

The grouping of subjects for picturesque effect, evidently illustrating fables or charades to be guessed, was an important feature of the original work which is practically lost. In many instances, however, the combination of certain figures proves of assistance in discovering the character of others. In the following sketch, supposed to represent Egypt, it begins with the Egyptian cross, said to be the earliest form of the cross used as a gibbet for the execution of criminals. Then we have the Pyramid and Obelisk, which pave the way for the introduction of the Sphynx and a crocodile, which under ordinary circumstances might not have been recognized.

The hieroglyphics show figures which are common to both Egyptian as well as Chinese inscriptions:

Regarding the spiritual or mythological interpretation of Chinese philosophy, which, as the Rev. Hamden C. DuBose has shown, defies all attempts at elucidation, the following specimen may be taken as being one of the most simple. It may possibly illustrate some fairy tale upon the lines of the Arabian Nights, but Professor Challenor has called attention to the fact of the six geometrical figures standing in the foreground as appearing in all editions of Tangrams as ancient designs of tombstones.

The upper part of the picture seems to represent a dark mountain, to which departed spirits are supposed to be flying, pursued by winged beasts, birds, and fishes. There appears to be a lake of water (or brimstone, perhaps), into which one human being has fallen, and is attempting to reach a typical Charon's barge. This is the only one, out of several score of weird pictures of this character, which is in any way self-explanatory or suggestive of a possible interpretation:

Regarding the scope of possibilities of Tangram designing it may be said that the same is bounded only by the imagination or audacity of its votaries. There is absolutely nothing too difficult to be essayed. The art of originating new designs is in its infancy, for, aside from the few impromptu figures here thrown together to elucidate the scheme, nothing has been added to the collection of designs for upward of 3,000 years.

An inexhaustible field stands practically unexplored, for it can certainly be said that 10,000 pictures, better than any here shown, can readily be designed. No one person, possibly, could make that number of fine pictures; it would consume too much time and no one's personal knowledge would be apt to extend over such a wide range of subjects. There is not a boy or girl in the land, however, who with a little practice cannot develop sufficient artistic ability to portray the familiar objects of their home life or surroundings with as correct or better fidelity than has been shown in these hastily thrown together illustrations. We are merely showing what can be done, and it is the perfect confidence in the thousands of others who can contribute better pictures than any here shown that induces the writer to volunteer to be *"The fool who will write the eighth book of Tan,"* which is to illustrate the progress of civilization up to the present day!

Such a collection does not of necessity have to be restricted to modern inventions, like the following array, which comes naturally to one's mind, showing a locomotive and a steamship; some pistols; a flying-machine chasing a balloon; a stereopticon, telephone, and phonograph, as well as a foundry, coal-breaker, machine-shops, and light-house:

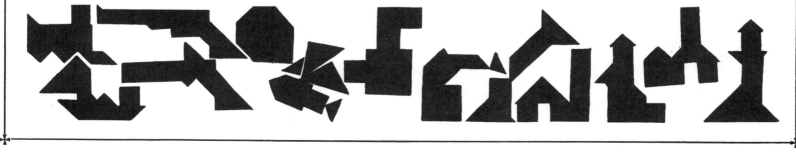

Modern civilization may be shown in a hundred different ways. By illustrating popular stories or fables; implements, trolley-cars or carriages, the changes of fashion, or any of the things seen in the ordinary affairs of life. Humorous tales may be told in pantomime, or we might portray fads or popular pastimes of the day. Here, for example, is a somewhat feeble attempt to illustrate a game of base-ball, wherein you may possibly recognize Casey at the bat, and Kelly's famous slide.

In the following view of a yacht race may be found a figure of a boat previously given to see if it could be recognized without explanatory remarks or accompanying pictures. It will be of interest to turn back and see what you supposed it to represent at the time. It is astonishing to find, after practicing with the Tangrams for some considerable time, with what facility we can see perfect designs in what had previously appeared to be utterly unintelligible:

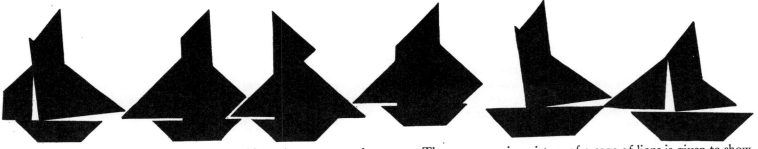

Animal studies which present the subjects in groups and various postures, as already shown, are to be recommended as calling attention to traits or characteristics which many might never have noticed or thought of before.

The accompanying picture of a cage of lions is given to show how the figures may be thrown in roughly, without any attempt at detail or artistic finish, if the attitudes and characteristics of the animals are sketched with sufficient boldness:

Enough has now been said to give an idea of the scope of the original works and of the marvellous possibilities of that feature of the pastime which pertains to our little school of design. It is to be hoped that the reader has reached that point of proficiency in the study of black and white when there is no further necessity for mentioning the names of the pictures, so we pass on with the graduating class, and study historical paintings to see who are deserving of diplomas. Does the following bit of canvas need any coloring to tell its own story? It is given in the nature of an illustrated puzzle.

In the sweet by and by, when the second part of the Eighth Book of Tan makes its appearance, there will be recognized an attempt to formulate a plan whereby all contributions, be they 1,000 or 10,000, shall be worked into some harmonious scheme worthy of the occasion. It must carry out the original idea so as to tell its great story in pantomime without resort to letterpress descriptions. Each and every person who contributes one or more designs worthy of a place in the book will have cause to be proud of the same and will receive a present of an autograph copy as a graduating diploma.

But circumstances alter cases, and "The best laid schemes o' mice and men gang aft agley." We may possibly illustrate one of those little Chinese plays which last for three years; nevertheless, there will be little groupings and side-plays galore, like the following four tableaux which are just clamoring for recognition:

From an artistic standpoint the following copy of the famous painting of "The Fox Hunters" would have been more realistic if a larger set of Tangrams had been used in the construction of the horses and riders, so as to give the correct relative proportions, as shown between the dogs and the fox. This pictorial effect is lacking in all modern editions:

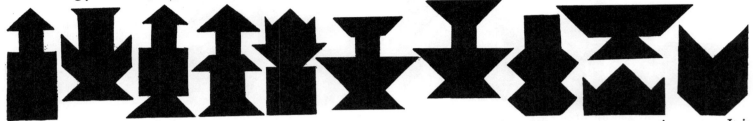

The Chinese are past masters in the matter of symmetry, and with the aid of Tangrams prove the truth of their old saying that "two ugly make a pretty." Any crooked, irregular line creates a beautiful and artistic design when duplicated in reverse, as if reflected in a mirror. Observe the lines on one side of any of the following figures and the result of duplicating the same.

Scattered through the original books are many little groupings of a disconnected character which do not appear to represent any particular point or narrative, fable or proverb, such as can be readily detected in other parts. These sketches undoubtedly conform harmoniously with the progressive development of the work, in that they introduce new costumes, pastimes, etc. It is believed, however, that they show the origin of an ancient but still popular style of Chinese picture-book for the young, which presents a number of illustrations for which the parents or some of the more clever children must invent appropriate stories:

Here is a slippery little scene, suggestive of wintry out-door sports on the ice and snow, with a fairly good representation of a Canadian tobogganing mishap. Space will not permit of placing the sketch properly bias-ways on the page, as occurs not unfrequently in the Chinese books, when, by a slight effort of the imagination, you might readily see them slide:

Despite of the careless or inaccurate manner of printing the designs in the original works, which is equivalent to giving imperfect data for a problem, there appears to be an over punctilious requirement for exact answers. So many changes are rung upon the slightest possible variation in a pattern, as if there were great merit in showing different ways of construction, that the same becomes monotonous. We can readily see how four designs can be produced by the slightest modification in the following

baptismal fonts, but it is not so easy to master the insignificant change necessary to alter the style of the Jockey's caps.

With the figures of the three cabinet organs we reach that borderland of mystery in the black art which can only be solved mathematically. The second and third organ in the original Chinese works are exactly alike; each is built from the same seven pieces, and yet the last one shows a folding lid which calls for an extra piece! Is this a fallacy or an optical illusion?

This paradoxical feature of Tangrams, whereby almost any of the geometrical forms appear to be susceptible of being constructed at pleasure with one piece more or less, is the great mystery referred to by ancient Chinese writers.

It has never been touched upon or even discovered by any writer within 2,000 years, although an important principle of Tangrams. Take the following magic dice-cup trick: Fig. 1 represents the cup, built with the seven pieces. Fig. 2 represents the same cup, of the same size, with a vacant space, although all the pieces are used! Observe that the third figure is also built

with the same pieces, but has a still smaller vacancy to fill. Of course it is a fallacy, a paradox, or an optical illusion, for you will say the feat is impossible! But look at the answers and see if any light is thrown on the subject!

Count the pieces and measure the dimensions carefully! The seventh and eighth figures represent the mysterious square, built with seven pieces; then with one corner clipped off, and still the same seven pieces employed. Explain this also, if you can, for there are greater mysteries yet to investigate!

Continuing our analysis of the square, rhomboid, or other geometrical shapes which can be constructed by the seven pieces, we find a paradoxical demonstration that the same forms may be built from either six, seven, or eight pieces!

The first three figures show imperfect designs containing seven pieces each, which might be completed by the addition of

an eighth piece, and yet we know that they can be made perfect with only seven pieces!

Strange to relate, the first of the figures is a famous puzzle, known as the Japanese Problem, the authorship of which has been claimed by several puzzlists and mathematicians. It is given in form of a square with one-ninth removed, and the conditions are to "discover how to divide the same into three pieces which will fit together and form a perfect square." It was a beautiful and difficult puzzle 3,000 years ago!

In Fig. 4 is given the answer to Fig. 1, showing how the same may be built with seven pieces, which would therefore require an eighth piece to complete, whereas we know that by a different arrangement the square can be made complete with only the seven!

The heavy white lines are given to show how to cut it into three pieces which will fit together and solve the Japanese problem.

In the same way in Fig. 5 is shown a perfect rhomboid constructed from the seven pieces, and yet in the next four designs are shown similar forms, each one containing the same seven pieces, although one of them appears to be missing, so that, as in Fig. 8, it would require nine pieces to make the form perfect.

We will now pry into the mysteries of the pyramids and ask the puzzlists and mathematicians to explain how it is possible to construct a perfect pyramid with seven pieces, or the imperfect ones, with one piece lacking, with the same number! It reminds one of the well-known story of the king who, in attempting to destroy one of the pyramids, removed one top stone, which the entire ability and resources of his nation could not restore. The encyclopædias say: "The Pyramids were built by the respective

kings for their own tombs, and were begun at the beginning of each reign, and their different sizes therefore correspond with the length of the reign." In which case they must have been constructed by the Irishman who knew how to put up the chimney first and then build down to the ground!

Two of the designs are marked off with white lines so as to show how to make a complete as well as an imperfect pyramid with the same seven pieces.

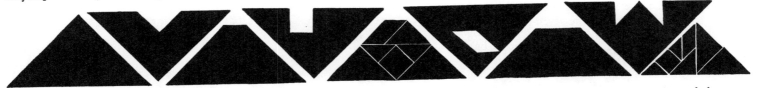

An examination of the second book of Tan shows that every figure there given is susceptible of being represented in two other forms; one a contraction and the other an extension, and that the expanded or extreme form produces the mysterious paradoxical principle of the missing piece.

Take, for example, the following shapes, to be found in all

modern collections, and note the different rendering of the same subject, as well as the trick of the vanishing piece shown in the second figure. By this paradoxical way of building it can be shown that some figures which contain seven pieces might be made with eight, or might also be built just as perfect with only six, so as to leave a piece to spare of any desired shape.

The mysterious changes do not pertain alone to the omission of certain pieces, but to numerous other paradoxical features, the fallacies of which are to be explained. In the Chinese books we find that the two versions of a spool are given with the lower one merely somewhat wider, which makes it an unsatisfactory answer to discover that the fallacy turns upon the lower flanges being larger, as shown. The disappearance of the upper flanges converts it into a jardinière, which is presented again with a piece chipped off.

In the next figure we see a mango flower sprouting, which speedily grows into quite a bush, and we have a complete exposition of the famous East India trick, with each tableau calling for all seven pieces. Then we have three representations of a bottle, which can be changed in several ways.

We next see three forms of the hexagon, which can be made to sprout, so that by a series of gradual changes we get a dagger, candle, obelisk, and tombstone. This evolutionary series is carried over on the next page.

Here are the familiar figures of the top-spinners, with a hitherto undiscovered interpretation. The first person is spinning the little top so as to place the ownership. Then we have a couple tossing the top between them, and the problem is to discover whether the top is one of the pieces belonging to the third or second figure, or an independent subject calling for seven more pieces. The three other figures are also cleverly placed so as to suggest a misleading answer to one of the best puzzles of the book.

Under the impression that all of the imperfect forms, which apparently lack one piece, were to be constructed from eight pieces, a foreign publisher, who was not up in puzzle matters, brought out a collection of designs which require one piece more, and furnished the same with a set of eight blocks! Each and every one of the problems can be constructed with seven, so, thanks to this happy blunder, some of the best figures known have been preserved. *Ne sutor ultra crepidam!*

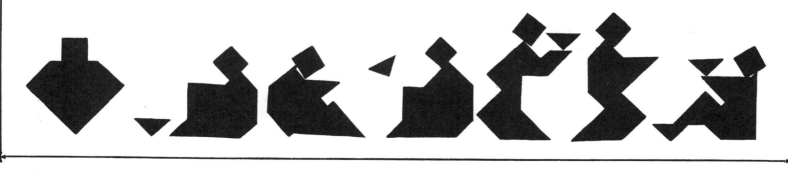

When it dawns upon us that there is something in Tangrams more closely allied to the exact sciences than to a simple pastime we discover that there is a mystery in the dimensions of the pieces somewhat akin to the marvellous measurements of the Pyramids, whose ninth power proved the sun to be 91,840,000 miles distant, when for thousands of years it was supposed to be less than 20,000. The proportions of the Pyramid showed the ratio of the diameter of a circle to its circumference, and also proved that the Egyptians knew the distance to the centre of the earth.

If you take an accurate rule and measure the dimensions of the following reproduction of the Tangram square it will prove to be $2\frac{1}{8}$ inches on its four sides. This being equivalent to $\frac{34}{16}$ of an inch, we get $34 \times 34 = 1,156$ as the square. The short sides of the largest pieces appear to be $\frac{24}{16}$ of an inch long, while the smaller pieces represent half of the dimensions, viz., $\frac{17}{16}$ and $\frac{12}{16}$. The four dimensions, therefore, are 34, 24, 17, and 12, and although it has been shown that the outside measurement 34×34 gives 1,156 as the area of the square, the measurement of the seven pieces computed separately makes it to be but 1,152! and the same is given as one of the unsolvable mysteries which Li Hung Chang said "cannot be explained."

The feature just described may throw some tangible light upon the Chinese philosophy quoted by Rev. Dr. Holt, which has been described by other writers as "pagan gibberish": "The illimitable produces the great extreme; the great extreme the two principles; the two principles produce the four dimensions, and the four dimensions develop what the Chinese call the eight diagrams of Feu-hi over 3,000 years ago."

The illimitable would thus be made to be the undiscovered pi of the square; the mysterious ratio of the sides of a square to its hypothenuse, just as in the diameter of the circle to its circumference.

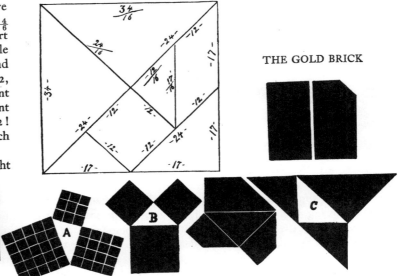

THE GOLD BRICK

The first of the above instalment of figures shows a mysterious change from one of the series of badges previously given, which paradoxical feat can only be appreciated by a careful study of the mathematics of Tangrams.

The second figure shows that a complete set of seven pieces forms a square, equal to sixteen triangles of the smaller size. The proportion, therefore, of the smallest piece to the whole set is what Mr. William Jennings Bryan would call the correct ratio of sixteen to one.

The small triangles, therefore, represent the unit value or one-sixteenth. The rhomboid piece, as well as the second size triangle and square, equal two-sixteenths each. The large triangles are equal to four-sixteenths.

In the puzzle of the two arrow-heads, given on page 32, the large one contains eleven-sixteenths and the smaller one five-sixteenths. Their relative proportions or sizes, therefore, are as 5 is to 11. A knowledge of this principle is absolutely necessary to solve some of the more difficult puzzles or to penetrate the mysterious features already discussed, as well as to determine the possibility of making some of the forms.

Chinese money, with the square, triangle, and rhomboid holes through the centre, was originally coined with certain values based upon the ratio of these Tangram shapes to the square.

That Tangrams were used in the teaching of mathematics is clearly shown by the presence of Euclid's famous 47th problem, known as *Pons Asinorum,* as shown in the above seventh figure, accompanied by simple kindergarten progressive steps.

"Tan" had two squares, the size of Fig. 3, which he desired to unite into one large square, so he cut one of the squares in two on the bias, and arranged the pieces in the form of a pyramid, as shown, and discovers that it forms half of a larger square. He then makes another pyramid from the other square and builds the square, which he knows to be exactly twice as large as the first, because it has twice as many pieces. Then he marked off a right-angled "corner" on a piece of paper and found that by placing the small squares on the sides and the large squares connecting them, so as to form the right-angled triangle B in the centre, he proved the proposition that when three squares form a right-angled triangle the largest square will be equal to the other two combined. Then he formulated the following invaluable rule of mechanics: when, having two squares of different sizes, it is required to find the dimensions of one square equal in area to the other two, draw a diagram of a right-angled corner, and measure off the diameter of one of the squares on one arm of the angle and the diameter of the other square on the other arm; then a straight line drawn from one of those points to the other,

forming the right-angled triangle A, will show the side of a square equal in area to the other two.

Then he found, as shown in Figs. 8 and 9, that this rule applied to polygons, triangles, circles, or any irregular shapes, so long as they were of the same form; viz., draw the right-angled corner, and upon one arm measure off a point which will indicate the shortest diameter of any irregular design. Then on the other arm measure off the shortest diameter of a larger representation of the same design, and the distance from one of those indicated points to that of the other arm will show the shortest diameter of an enlargement of the design equal to the other two. All of which was known many, many thousands of years ago.

This brief reference to the mathematics of Tangrams shows how Li Hung Chang would have the book interpreted according to the age and mental calibre of the students.

The working out of Tangram puzzles and the originating of new designs fills the long-felt want for a refined and instructive relaxation from overwork, as well as a good antidote for ennui.

Tangram parties become very enjoyable when sets of pieces with full instructions are sent out with the invitations a couple of weeks in advance, requesting the guests to furnish a number of original designs, unaccompanied by descriptions or names of authors; the intention being for an impromptu art committee to award some humorous prize for the best work.

By this plan, it may be mentioned, some choice and interesting contributions to the Eighth Book of Tan have been secured from some very distinguished sources.

Now, scholars, run away and amuse yourselves, for I am invited to say a few words to the children of a larger growth.

THE UNSOLVED PROBLEMS

The Second Book of Tan, like the lost Euclid, was given to elementary problems, the correctness or fallacy in the construction of which was to be discovered by the student, who was required to decide between the correctness of two conflicting propositions. The squaring of the circle appears to have been treated according to the following kindergarten method, which will furnish food for reflection for the young folks as well as the brainy mathematicians.

To make it clear to all, it may be explained that the squaring of the circle is merely the problem of figuring out how many square feet are contained in a circle of a given diameter—viz., how many square feet of sod are there in a round grass-plot 100 feet in diameter?

"If the *Pons Asinorum*, as shown, is correct," says Tan, "let us describe these semicircles upon the sides of the triangle *A*. Knowing that *B* is equal to *C* and *D* combined in Fig. 1, we will divide *B* by a straight cut from *X* to *Z*. Then the remaining half of *B*, as shown in Fig. 2, will be equal in area to *C*.

"Let us now, as shown in Fig. 3, continue the circle from *X* to *Z* and draw the vertical line from *X* to *Y* so as to cut the semicircular pieces *D* and *D* from both *C* and *B*. Those pieces which are removed being exactly similar, taken from forms of the same areas, prove that the remainders *C* and *B* must be of the same areas, although the one is a triangle and the other a crescent.

"The space *A* being of similar size and construction to *B* we proceed to place the pieces as shown in Fig. 4 and halve them by a straight cut from *C* to *X*, so as to have the remaining pieces as shown in Fig. 5, which have been proven by construction to be of the same areas.

"We will then cut the piece *C* by a diagonal line, and, as shown by the dotted lines, proceed to describe the circle enclosed within a square.

"Now let us show by analysis what has been proven: *CC* have been shown by Figs. 3, 4, and 5 to be equal to *A*.

"As *BB* added to *CC* would form a square of the same size as *AD*, then *BB* must be equal to *D*, as *CC* are equal to *A*. It shows that *B* must be equal to *B* and *C* equal to *C*, because *BB* equals *A* or *BC* equals *A*.

"Then if the segments *B*, *B*, *C*, and *C* are all equal, each piece represents the sixteenth part of the large square, and we find that *twelve of these sixteen pieces are contained within the circle*.

"Therefore, if the square is 100 in diameter, 100 × 100 = 10,000 square feet, of which our grass-plot, which was said to be 100 feet in diameter, would contain twelve-sixteenths, or just 7,500 square feet!"

And, as Tan says, "There you are! the truth or fallacy of *Pons Asinorum* is submitted to the judgment of the students who will kindly pass in their examination papers to the professor."

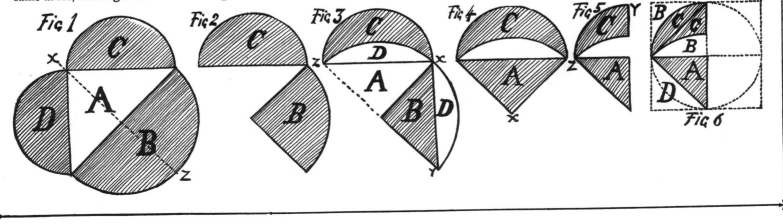

The *tri-section of an angle* is the most interesting of the unsolved problems of mathematics, because of the extreme simplicity of the proposition: "How can you divide any given angle into three equal parts?"

Here is the way to bisect an angle so as to divide it into two parts: Take any angle formed by the junction of two straight lines, and with the leg of the compasses placed at *A* mark off the arc *BB.* Then place the compasses on *B* and *B,* describe the arcs *C* and *C,* and a straight line drawn from the intersection of these two arcs to *A* bisects the angle.

Now discover how to trisect the angle by rule without recourse to experimental measurements.

In mechanical practice we should describe the semicircle *BB,* as shown in Fig. 2, and by trial measurements find approximately correct points for *C* and *D.* At the first glance it would seem as if by laying off the three arcs respectively one, two, and three inches from *A* as shown, that *B* is exactly three times as large as *E.* Such actually is the case, but, as the curves of the two circumferences are different, we can find no way to measure that of the smaller upon the greater, as shown by *F.*

F is the same as the arc *E,* and if it could be represented by a strip of flexible paper which accommodates itself to the form of the arc *BB,* we would readily locate the point.

The problem is a fascinating one, which has interested all mathematicians from the time of Archimedes, Pythagoras, Euclid, and Euler to the present day, although a simple one, which can be solved readily by rule and compass alone, and might be guessed by any bright little boy or girl.

The writer is prepared to show that the answer was known to the ancients many thousand years ago, and a simple demonstration of the method of getting a correct answer has been passed upon as correct and absolutely satisfactory by the highest mathematical authority of the present day.

The interest which clings to the problem of trisecting the angle turns upon the fact of such a simple proposition, demolishing the great axiom that a good rule should work both ways.

Any measurement repeated three times furnishes an angle correctly trisected, but if we start from the larger angle first no rule has yet been discovered which will work backwards so as to trisect it.

Take three pieces of Tangrams and place them together, and we find they show the angle of 135 degrees properly trisected; but how is it possible to work the other way so as to divide any given angle into three parts?

The accompanying Tangram illustration shows the four lines converging to one point:

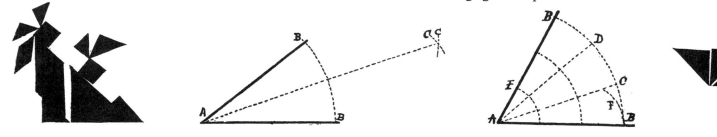

Continuing from the last figure of the tombstone, given a few pages back, we can construct the same so as to have a small piece to spare. This piece may be sprouted into a new design, and then led into a form of cup, and from that into a vase of artistic shape. That triangular piece will make a pestle for a mortar, which might readily be transformed into a goose, etc.

In attempting to construct a form like the imperfect hexa-gon shown, it can be seen that the square will not fit, but we are on the right track, because having just sufficient material left over proves the proportions to be correct. Have you thought of the ratio or proportion of one piece or form to another?

Do you see the Monad sign which says, go back to the beginning and read over again! Note the little lamp of science with a modern Argand burner on the end of it!

The feature of leading the imagination to recognize certain forms by their connection with others may be referred to again as pertaining to some amusing tricks, which appear more in the nature of catches. It will be found that many of the repetitions which have been adversely criticised are merely the reappearance of former designs under different aspects. They look as if some-one in search of original ideas had glanced through the pages with the book turned upside down to get new suggestions.

Here, for instance, we have a monkey-wrench, and directly under it an improved one with a set-screw. Then we have a pretty Japanese girl, with a figure below showing how her bustle will appear when she makes a graceful salaam. Next comes a light carriage with a top, and below it is shown the same style with the hind wheels larger, as they should be. Now, if you look at the three lower designs of the wrench, Japanese girl, and car-riage, you see the one design reproduced three times.

In the sketch of the Irishman with a wheelbarrow it does not require close examination to discover the similarity.

There is somewhat of magic involved in the happy family of pigs which might possibly be overlooked. That first mis-chievous looking "razor-back" is somewhat out of proportions in the hind quarters. Directly below him is an improvement, which gains a tail but is rather light chested. The top one at the end is the best, and we are asked to compare it with the last, which seems to have acquired a tail by some magical means, which really makes it look more like a rat, which, according to the principles of Chinese evolution, suffices to prove their close relationship. The problem is to explain how the pig comes by that tail.

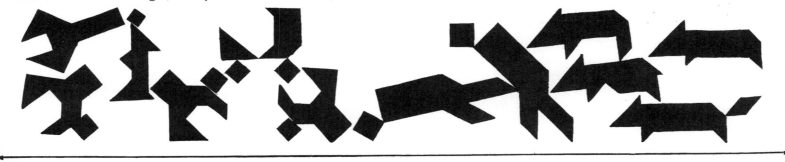

SOLUTIONS

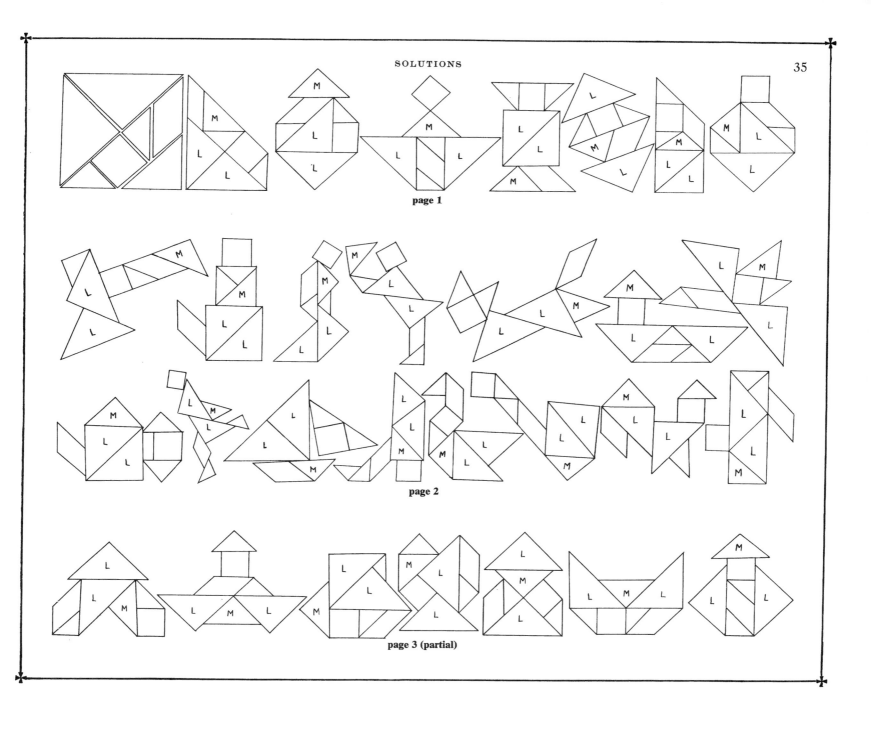

page 1

page 2

page 3 (partial)

SOLUTIONS

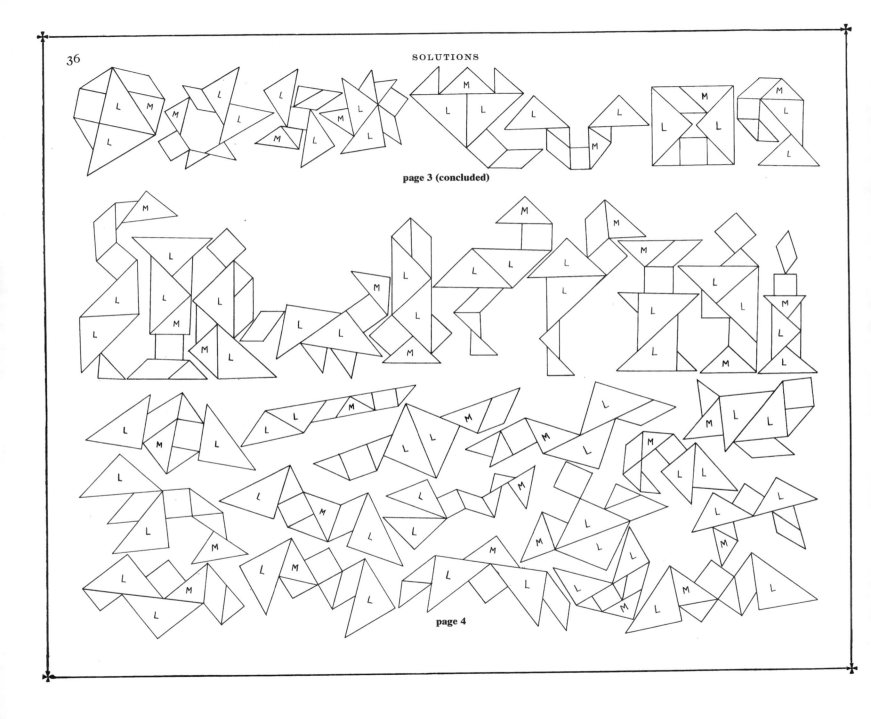

page 3 (concluded)

page 4

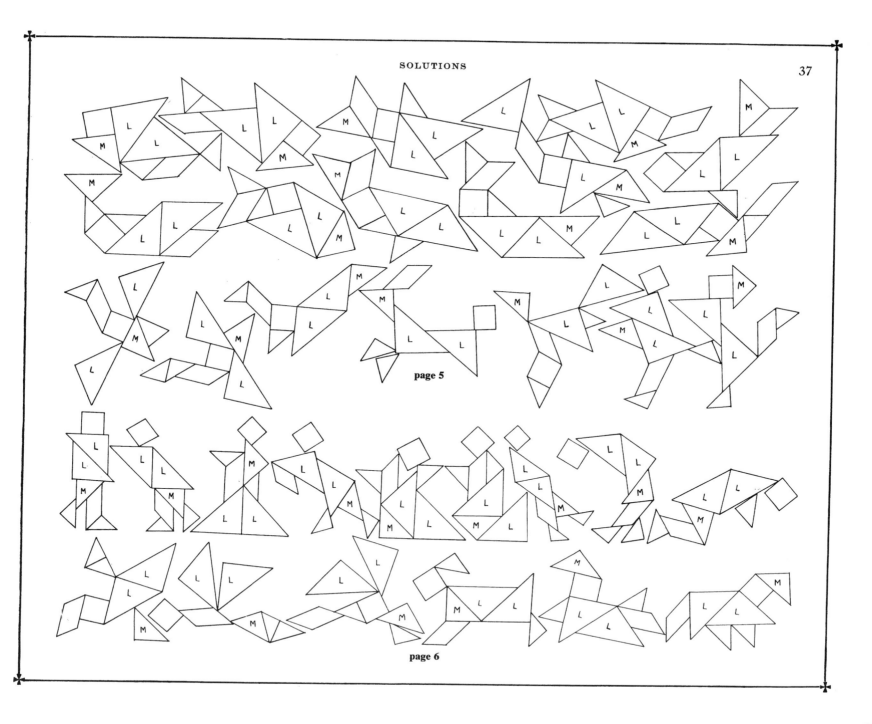

page 5

page 6

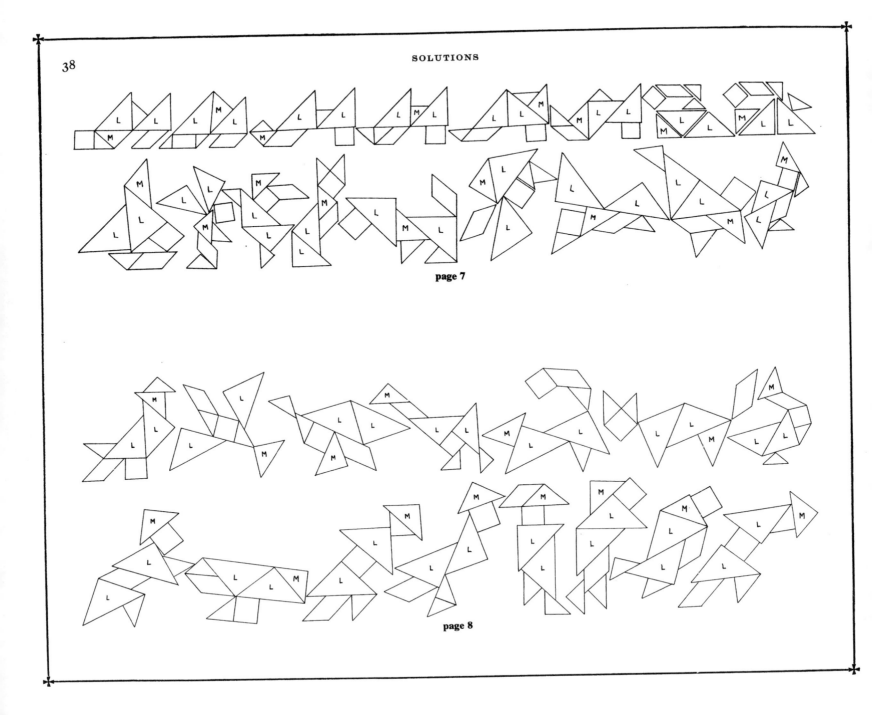

page 7

page 8

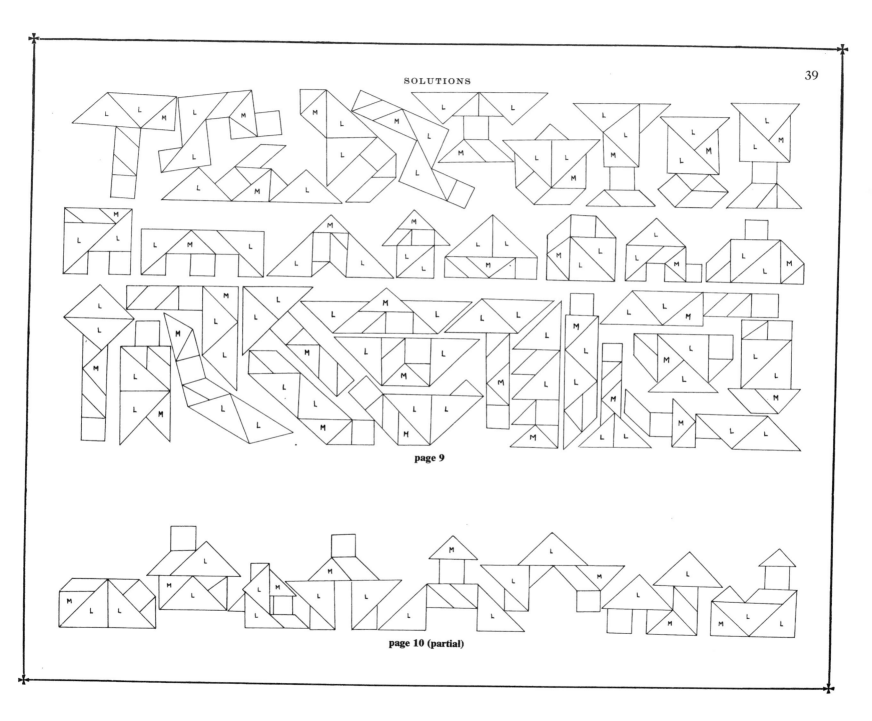

page 9

page 10 (partial)

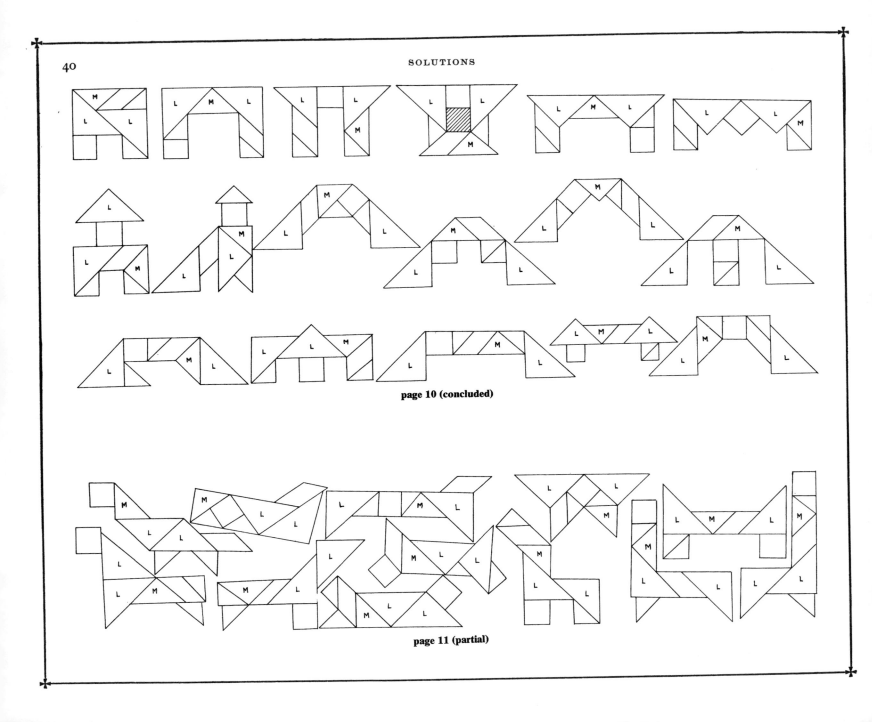

page 10 (concluded)

page 11 (partial)

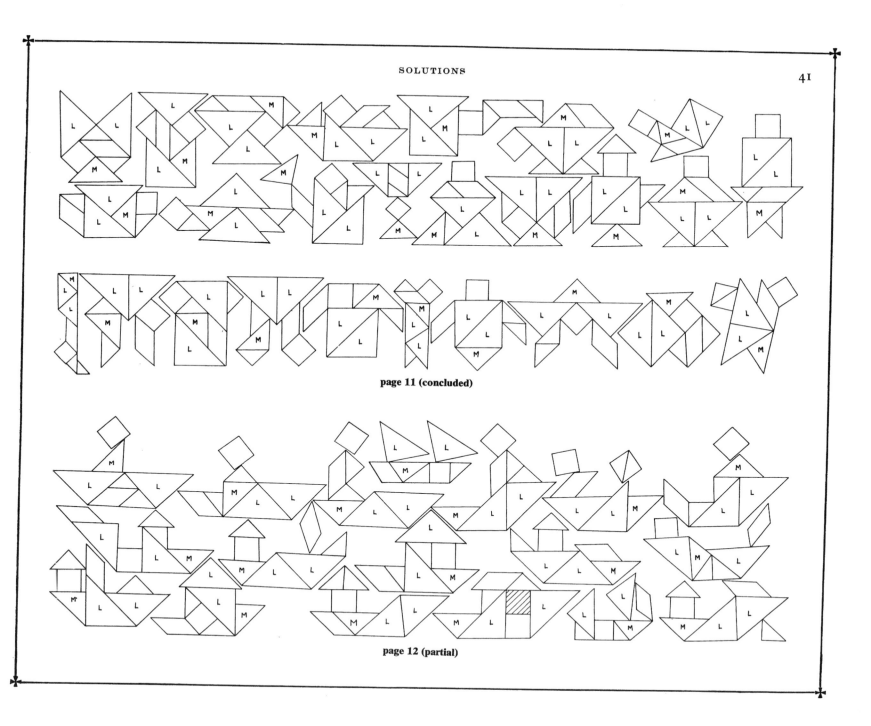

page 11 (concluded)

page 12 (partial)

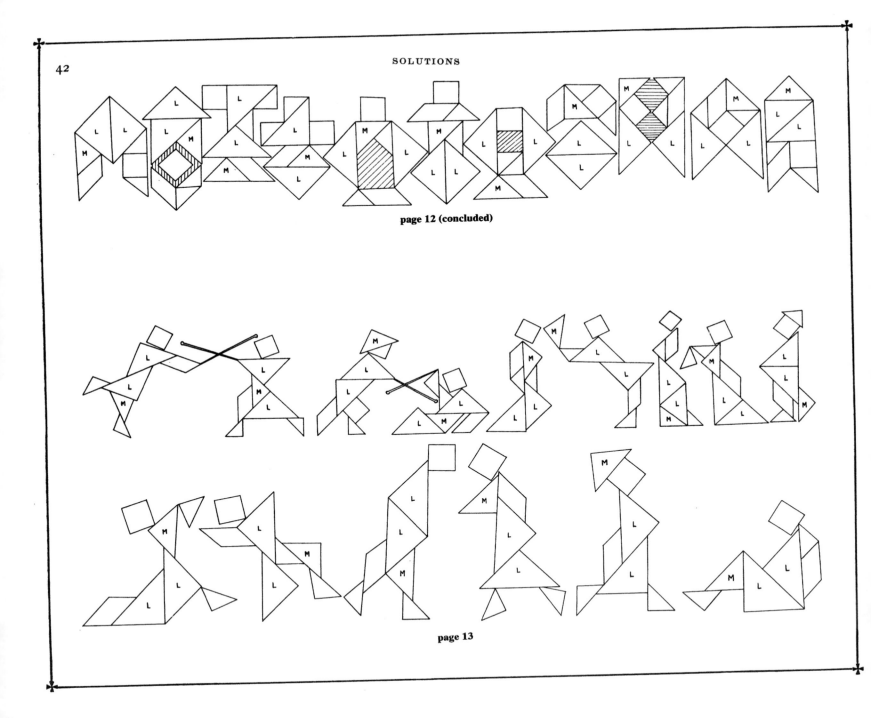

page 12 (concluded)

page 13

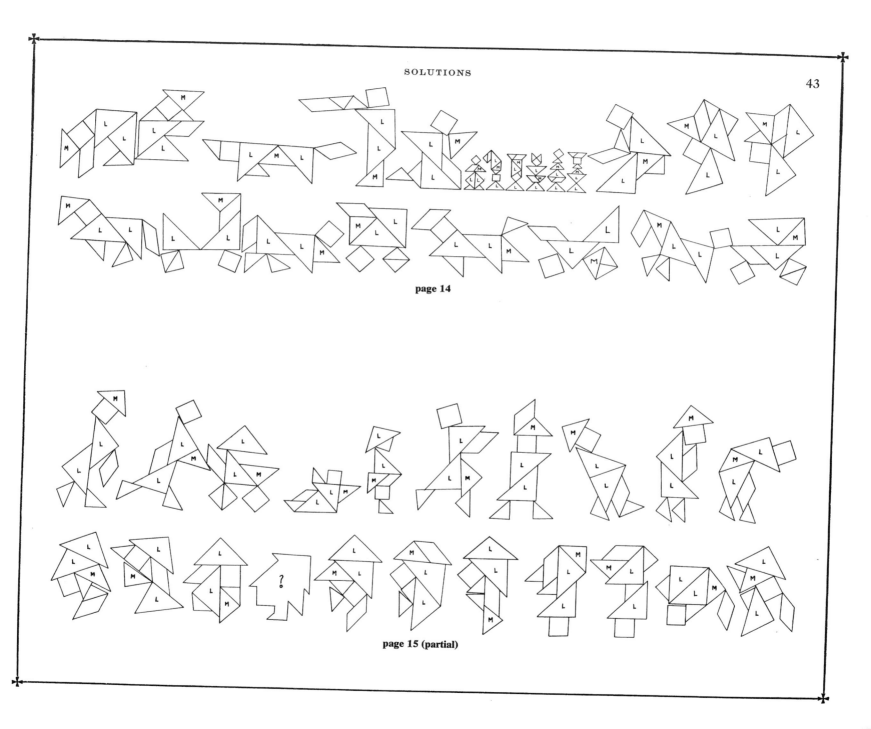

page 14

page 15 (partial)

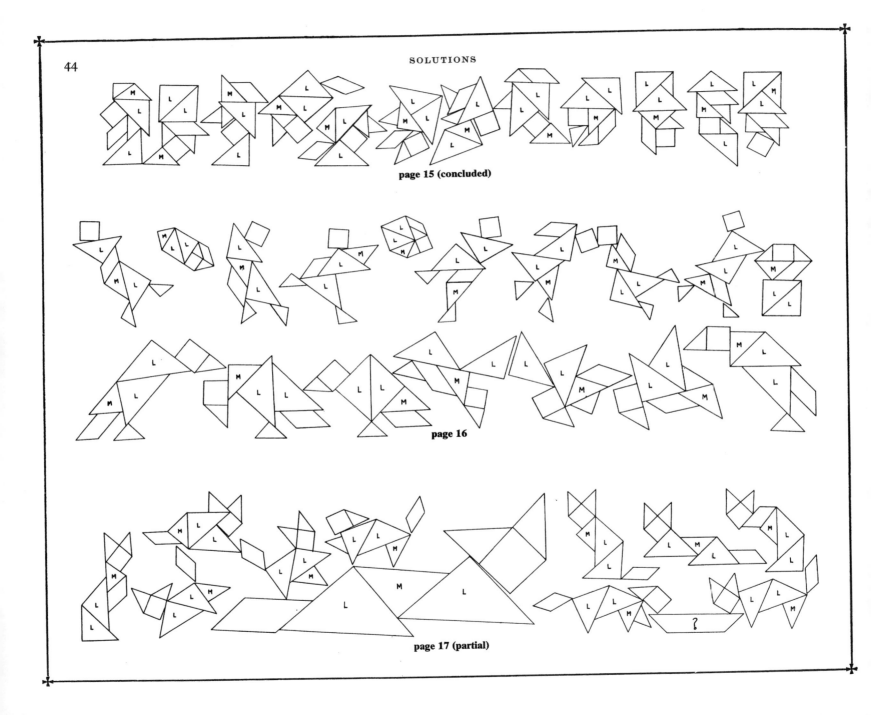

page 15 (concluded)

page 16

page 17 (partial)

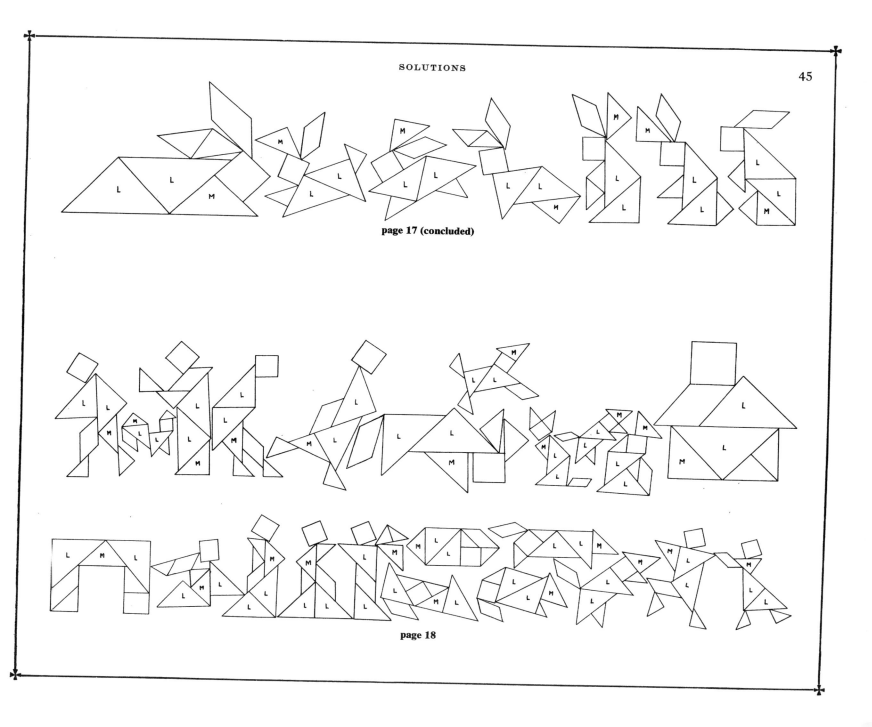

page 17 (concluded)

page 18

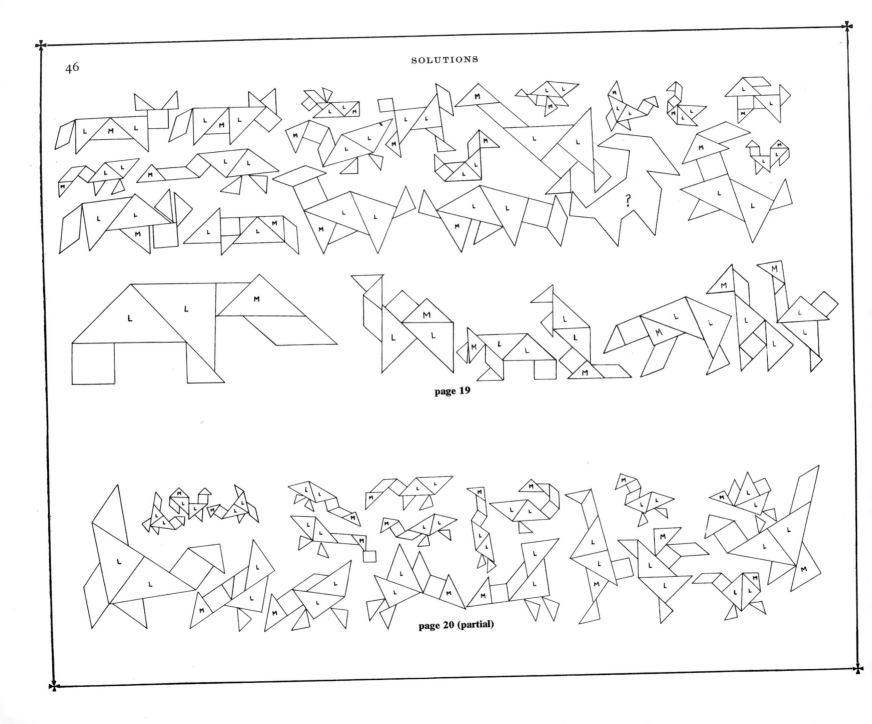

page 19

page 20 (partial)

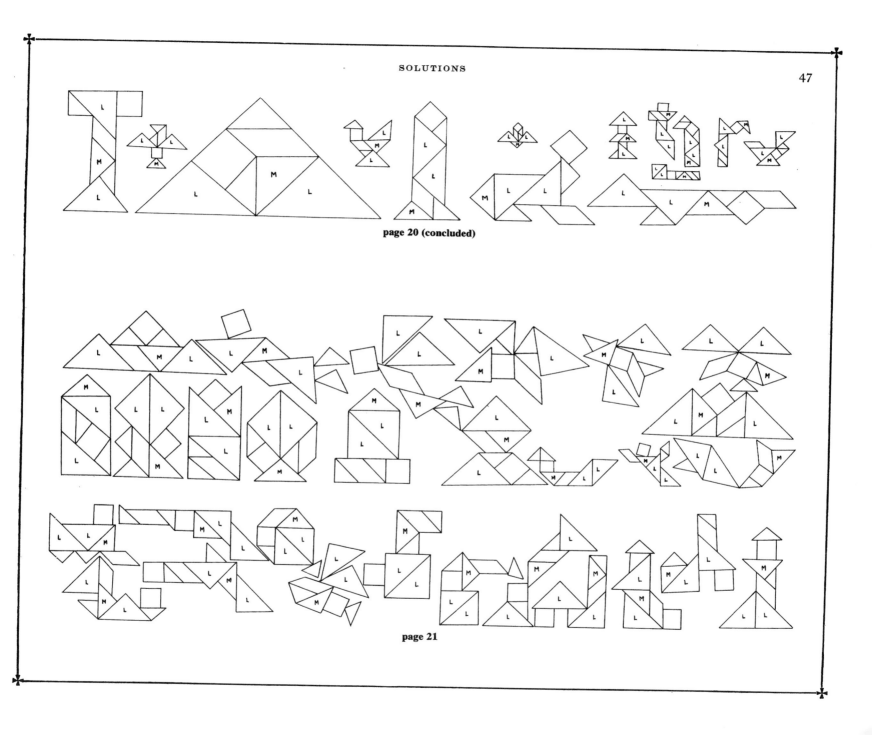

page 20 (concluded)

page 21

48

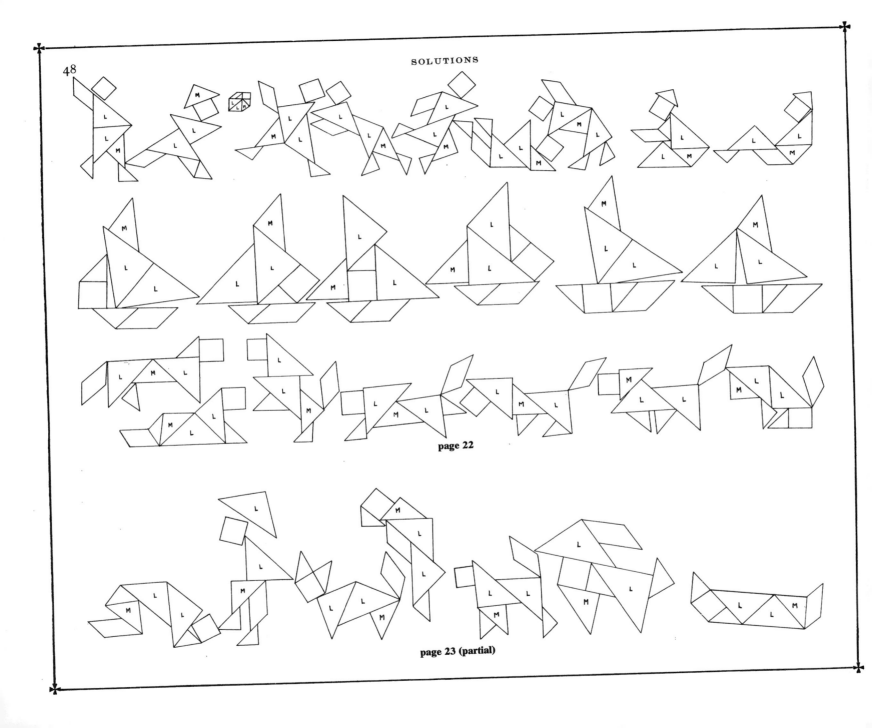

page 22

page 23 (partial)

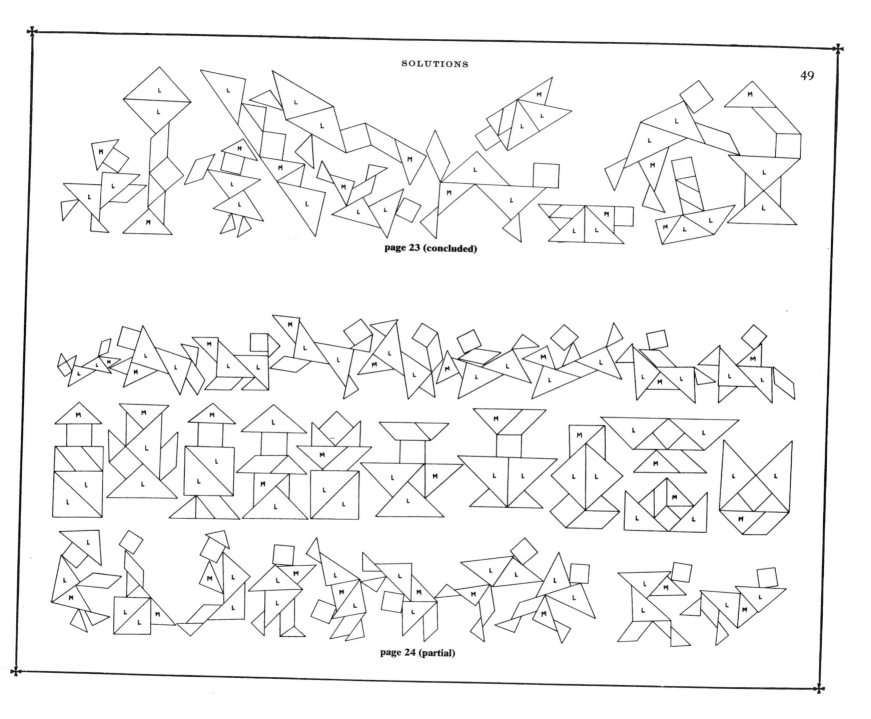

page 23 (concluded)

page 24 (partial)

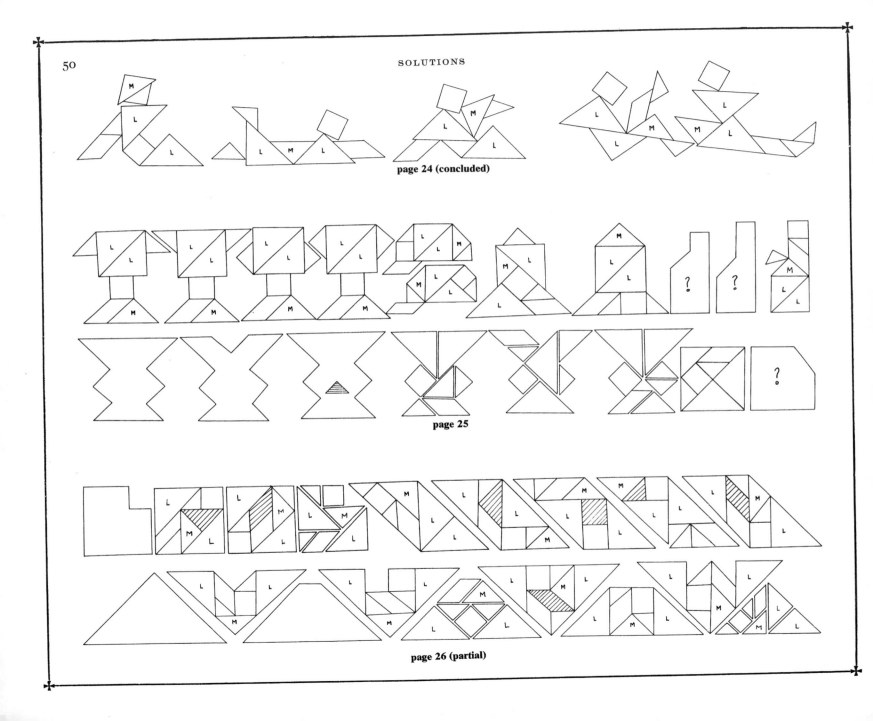

page 24 (concluded)

page 25

page 26 (partial)

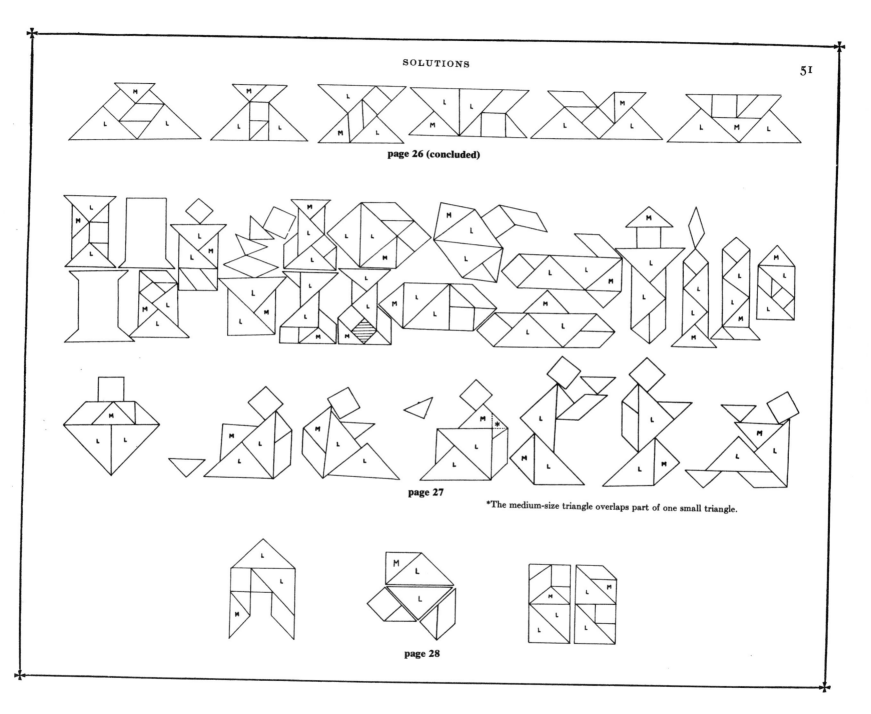

page 26 (concluded)

page 27

*The medium-size triangle overlaps part of one small triangle.

page 28

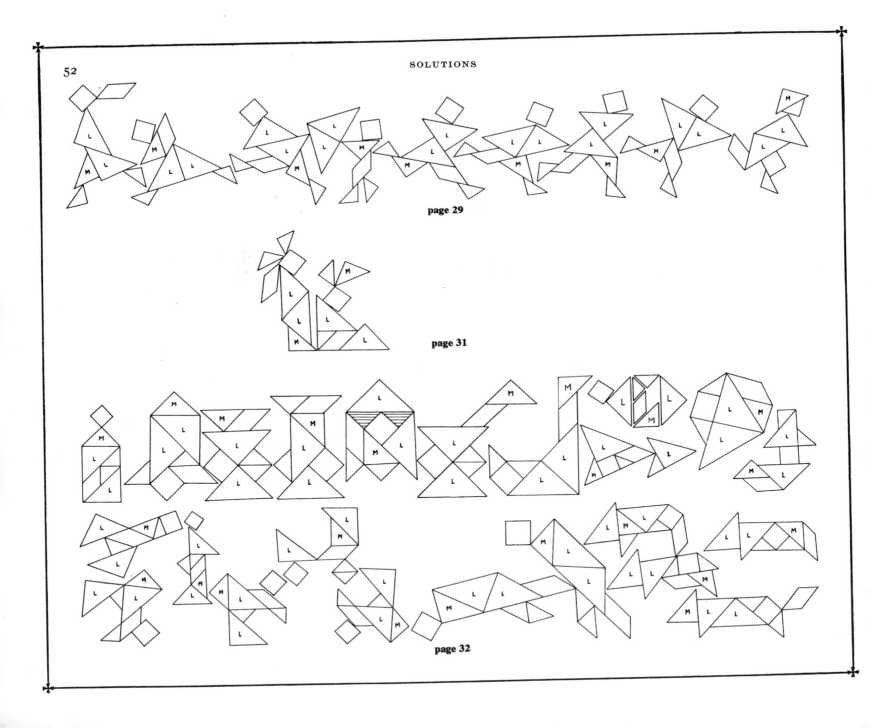

page 29

page 31

page 32